DEDICATION

My mom has always loved to go places; the destination was not all that important to her—she just liked to go somewhere. Never mastering the art of driving a car, she chose to walk a great deal. In my early years there was no hesitation in towing me along on countless adventures through the streets of Portland, my tiny legs working double time in a desperate attempt to keep up with her grown-up pace. Those times now far behind, this book is dedicated to Audrey L. White, for passing on to her son a fondness for walking and for instilling that urge to discover what's around the next bend.

Snowshoe
Trails of
Yosemite

Michael C. White

WILDERNESS PRESS
BERKELEY

First Edition November 1999

Copyright © 1999 by Michael C. White
Photographs by the author except where noted
All maps © 1999 by Wildflower Productions with trails added
    by the author

Book design by Jaan Hitt
Cover design by Larry B. Van Dyke
Front cover photo: View from Dewey Point © 1999 by Michael C. White

Library of Congress Card Catalog Number 99-052276
ISBN 0-89997-253-5

Manufactured in the United States of America

Published by **Wilderness Press**
             1200 5th Street
             Berkeley, CA 94710
             (800) 443-7227; FAX (510) 558-1696
             mail@wildernesspress.com

Contact us for a free catalog
Visit our web site at www.wildernesspress.com

Printed on recycled paper, 20% post-consumer waste

Library of Congress Cataloging-in-Publication Data
White, Michael C., 1952-
        Snowshoe trails of Yosemite/ Michael C. White.--1st ed.
        p.cm.
        Includes bibliographical references (p.) and index.
        ISBN 0-89997-253-5 (alk. paper)
        1. Snowshoes and snowshoeing--California--Yosemite National
Park--Guidebooks. 2. Cross-country ski trails--California--Yosemite
National Park--Guidebooks. 3. Yosemite National Park (Calif)--
Guidebooks. I. Title.

GV853 .W57 1999
917.94'470453--dc21   99-052276

TABLE OF CONTENTS

I. General Information

II. Trips

Contents

III. Appendices

Read This

Snowshoeing in the backcountry entails unavoidable risk that every snowshoer assumes and must be aware of and respect. The fact that a trail is described in this book is not a representation that it will be safe for you. Trails vary greatly in difficulty and in the degree of conditioning and agility one needs to enjoy them safely. On some trips routes may have changed or conditions may have deteriorated since the descriptions were written. Also trail conditions can change even from day to day, owing to weather and other factors. A trail that is safe on a clear day or for a highly conditioned, agile, properly equipped snowshoer may be completely unsafe for someone else or unsafe under adverse weather conditions.

You can minimize your risks on the trail by being knowledgeable, prepared and alert. There is limited space in this book for a general treatise on safety in the mountains, but there are a number of more thorough good books and public courses on the subject and you should take advantage of them to increase your knowledge. Just as important, you should always be aware of your own limitations and of conditions existing when and where you are snowshoeing. If conditions are dangerous, or if you're not prepared to deal with them safely, choose a different trip! It's better to have wasted a drive than to be the subject of a mountain rescue.

These warnings are not intended to scare you off the trails. However, one element of the beauty, freedom, and excitement of the wilderness is the presence of risks that do not confront us at home. When you snowshoe you assume those risks. They can be met safely, but only if you exercise your own independent judgement and common sense.

Trips in this Book

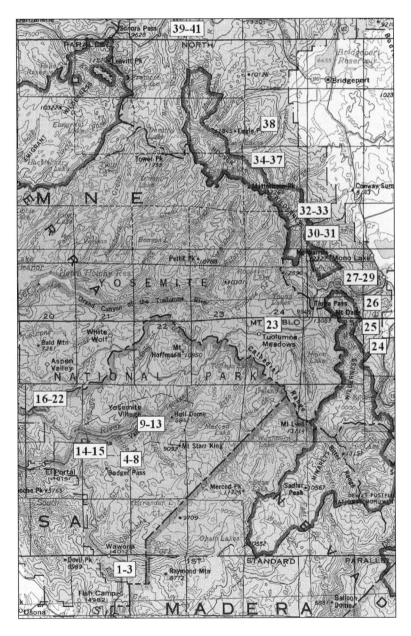

Giant Sequoia

CHAPTER 1

INTRODUCTION

Anyone who has seen a print of Ansel Adam's famous photograph, *Clearing Winter Storm*, knows the stunning beauty inherent to Yosemite Valley after a fresh blanket of snow carpets the valley floor and dusts the granite walls of the canyon. In the photograph, viewers are held captive by breaking clouds and the interplay of winter's light on a part of the Valley through gaps in the overcast sky. Ironically, the way most admirers experience the winter majesty of Yosemite is vicariously, through just such a photograph rather than first-hand. As in a number of America's national parks, winter is the off-season for visitation at California's most prestigious natural wonder. While Park revenues may decline as the days grow shorter, winter recreationists in quest of Yosemite's snowy mountain splendor can enjoy the relative tranquillity, without the usual hordes of tourists common to the Park in the warmer seasons. While surrounded by the awesome beauty of such extraordinarily popular landmarks as El Capitan and Half Dome, snowshoers have the rich blessing of listening only to the crunch of their own snowshoes upon the sparkling snow of Yosemite's winter landscape.

Most people upon hearing the term "Yosemite" think primari-

1

ly of Yosemite Valley, where the majority of visitors to the Park spend their time. However, Yosemite National Park is made up of much more than just the Valley. Encompassing almost 760,000 acres and ranging in elevation from 2,000 to over 13,000 feet, the Park is grand in scope and rich in diversity. Designated wilderness makes up 94% of the land within the Park boundaries, providing a nearly inexhaustible range of opportunities for backcountry exploration.

When the first significant snowfall blankets the upper reaches of the Park in late autumn or early winter, the backcountry expands as roads are closed and entry points for the high country are forced down to lower elevations. The snow line creeps down from the upper regions of the Park toward the Valley as winter progresses, prohibiting auto-bound sightseers from visiting such popular summer destinations as Tuolumne Meadows and Glacier Point. The loss of access for most people quickly becomes a bonus for the much smaller percentage of those Yosemite devotees who are willing to power themselves on snowshoes or skis. People possessing plenty of time and blessed with satisfactory weather, can now roam the Yosemite countryside to their heart's content. The number of opportunities for snowshoe enthusiasts to practice their art blossoms as the winter solstice heralds the arrival of the winter season.

Variations in snow conditions are the norm for Yosemite Valley over the course of an average winter, confounding the planning process for snowshoe or ski trips on the Valley floor. Successful adventures based on the quality of the snow are more a matter of serendipity or fate. However, besides the Valley Yosemite has three developed areas of more consistent snow quality and quantity, as well as a nearly unlimited backcountry ripe for exploration by adventurous snowshoers. Crane Flat, Mariposa Grove and Badger Pass all have a number of marked and unmarked trails for both skiers and snowshoers. A number of other access points spread around the Park provide winter enthusiasts with gateways into the expansive Yosemite wilderness. Just outside the east Park boundary, additional terrain invites discovery from various points along US Highway 395.

Native Americans had dwelt for many centuries in the bountiful valley wedged between precipitous granite cliffs that would someday be known as Yosemite, but the first Caucasians to actually step foot into Yosemite Valley were the men of the Mariposa Battalion under the command of Major James Savage. Charged with the task of tracking down renegade Indians unwilling to accept life on a reservation near Fresno (can you blame them?), 58 enlisted men and officers traveled into the Valley in March of 1851. While most of the soldiers were unimpressed by their surroundings, Lafayette Bunnell, was affected to the point of recording the journey. Thanks to the Yosemite Association reprint in 1990, modern-day readers can relive Bunnell's vivid account of an undeveloped Yosemite Valley in *Discovery of the Yosemite*.

Around a campfire during the Mariposa Battalion foray, Dr. Bunnell suggested the valley should be named after the Indians who inhabited the region. Because of the mistaken idea that they were the Yo-sem-it-y tribe, the Valley was so christened. By the time the tribe's real name of Ah-wah-ne-chee was discovered, the incorrect appellation was irrevocably fixed in the minds of white men, and it was later modified to the current spelling.

Once it was discovered, Yosemite Valley's acclaim began to grow rapidly. By 1857 the first primitive hotel was erected. The same year Galen Clark, who would become the Park's first guardian, arrived in the Wawona area. In 1864, in the aftermath of a flurry of private acquisitions, the federal government granted Yosemite Valley and the Mariposa Grove of Big Trees to the state of California to "be held for public use, resort, and recreation." Such a grant marked the beginning of our National Park system. As Yosemite's reputation grew and transportation to the Valley became more accessible, more and more travelers came to see the giant trees, spectacular waterfalls, and sheer granite cliffs towering 3,000 feet and more above the valley floor.

Despite the initial park status, during the 1870's and '80's, parts of the greater Yosemite region were being environmentally undermined by excessive tourism, extensive logging, and overgrazing by sheep. To counteract these attacks, Congress in 1890 placed an area containing the watersheds around Yosemite Valley into federal hands under National Park jurisdiction, administered by the Fourth Cavalry. While the Cavalry had some success routing sheepherders, they were unable to solve the increasing number of problems in

Yosemite Valley, since those lands remained under state control. Thanks to the influence of John Muir and the Sierra Club, in 1906 Congress passed a bill absorbing the lands of Yosemite Valley back into the federal protection of Yosemite National Park.

After a fairly admirable stint, the Fourth Cavalry was relieved of its duties in Yosemite in 1916. The National Park Service was then faced with adapting the Park to suit a more mobile clientele, thanks at first to the transcontinental railroad and then to the advent of the private automobile. For the rest of this century, most of the major challenges the Service faced had to do with the pressures of increased visitation. After World War II, more and more visitors came to Yosemite each year, increasing the pressure on the Park's resources. Prior to the 1970's most of the Park Service's concerns involved improving the infrastructure of Yosemite. Then, the energy shifted toward reducing the adverse impact of an increasing number of visitors and their automobiles. Plans have been proposed and new initiatives adopted along the way, but the number of visitors to Yosemite continues to increase. The challenge of managing the Park continues, and for the foreseeable future will remain the most significant problem for Yosemite's modern-day guardians.

Winter provides the recreationist with the best chance for an uncrowded visit to the Park. Gone are the summer hordes and the resulting traffic jams, endless lines at Valley facilities, and quotas for backcountry trails. Winter is certainly the most peaceful season in Yosemite Valley and, with a few exceptions, the remainder of the Park is downright deserted. The eastern fringe of the high Sierra sees very few winter visitors as well. For recreationists seeking a refreshingly quiet Yosemite experience, there is no better opportunity than on a pair of snowshoes.

ACCESS

Except for periodic closures due to heavy amounts of snowfall from Pacific storms, all three state highways leading into Yosemite National Park originating from the valleys on the west side of the Sierra remain open during winter. Motorists traveling from the south can enter the park at the South Entrance near Wawona via Highway 41 from Fresno. Commonly referred to inside the Park as the Wawona Road, this route provides access to the Mariposa Grove Winter Trails area, located just beyond the entrance station. Beyond this South Entrance, the Wawona Road climbs 17 miles to a high point at Chinquapin and a junction with the Glacier Point Road (providing access to Badger Pass), before descending another 8 ½ miles to Yosemite Valley. Just before reaching the valley floor near Bridalveil Fall, motorists can marvel at the impressive vista of the valley from Discovery View, immediately after the Wawona Tunnel.

From the town of Merced, visitors can follow the Merced River on a winding course along Highway 140 to the Arch Rock Entrance near El Portal. Within the Park this highway is referred to as the El Portal Road. Beyond the entrance station, the El Portal Road continues to follow the river for another 5 miles to junctions with the Big Oak Flat and Wawona roads and then on into Yosemite Valley.

The northernmost route into the park is Highway 120 from Manteca, passing into Yosemite at the Big Oak Flat entrance. Known as the Big Oak Flat Road, this route climbs 7 ½ miles from the entrance station to a junction at Crane Flat (providing access to the Crane Flat Winter Trails area). While Highway 120 officially becomes the Tioga Road at this junction, the Big Oak Flat Road continues for 9 more miles to a junction with the main route into Yosemite Valley.

Eventually, all three highways lead to the same road into Yosemite Valley. All drivers will ultimately enter the valley on Southside Drive, the two-lane, one-way road that heads east past Bridalveil Fall, Yosemite Chapel and LeConte Memorial on the way to Curry Village. Westbound motorists will follow Northside Road past Yosemite Village and Yosemite Lodge on their way out of the valley. Gasoline is no longer available in the Valley, so be sure to fill up before getting there. Gas can be obtained within the Park at Crane Flat and Wawona; otherwise fill up in one of the towns outside the Park.

Snowfall is sporadic in Yosemite Valley, but winter visitors should carry tire chains at all times. Chains or 4-wheel drive with snow-tire requirements may be posted, and enforced, at any time. In addition, chain controls are in effect much of the winter for access to

Badger Pass. Bear in mind that the 5-mile section of Glacier Point Road from the Wawona Road to Badger Pass is open only when the ski area is operating, typically closing after Easter weekend.

Within the Park, winter snows do close two of the highways that summer visitors frequently use to access famous attractions. The Tioga Road, which takes motorists from June through October on a scenic 50-mile journey to Tuolumne Meadows and then on to Tioga Pass, is closed ½ mile from the Crane Flat junction. The Crane Flat Winter Trails area is at this location, providing winter enthusiasts with a number of routes for skiing or snowshoeing. The other significant road closure is at Badger Pass, 5 miles from the junction with the Wawona Road at Chinquapin, beyond which the Glacier Point Road is no longer plowed. During the months of heaviest visitation, sightseers travel 30 miles up this road to Glacier Point and the world-famous views of Yosemite landmarks. In winter, the Badger Pass area also provides access for skiers and snowshoers to these views and a vast range of other recreational opportunities.

Access to the backcountry along the east fringe of Yosemite is provided by US Highway 395. Aside from storm closures, this north-south thoroughfare remains open during the winter, allowing links from Los Angeles to Bishop, Mammoth Lakes and Reno. The only access from US 395 into the Park is just outside the small town of Lee Vining, where State Highway 120 heads west toward Tioga Pass. For about five months of the year, this route is the highest automobile road in California, cresting the Sierra at 9,945 feet. However, Highway 120 is closed just a few miles west of the Lee Vining junction in winter.

Travelers along US 395 will encounter a number of passes en route to their potential destinations. From south to north, motorists may have to negotiate Deadman, Conway and Devils Gate Summits, the first two above 8,000 feet and the latter near 7,500. During the winter, all vehicles should carry tire chains, as they may be required during and after winter storms.

While many commercial establishments along US 395 close up for the winter or greatly reduce their hours, gasoline can still be had in the towns of Mammoth Lakes, June Lake, Lee Vining and Bridgeport. However, be prepared to pay top dollar.

From US 395 a variety of Forest Service roads branch off to the west toward the mountains of the eastern Sierra, allowing outdoor enthusiasts access to the backcountry. The condition of these roads is highly variable during winter. As the snow line fluctuates up and down the mountainsides during the course of the winter, drivers may be able to travel far up into the hills before donning snowshoes or they may be forced to begin at the shoulder of US 395.

TRANSPORTATION

Automobiles

As in most recreation areas of the West, access to the snowshoe trails described in this book is primarily by private automobile. Ongoing discussions concerning the environmental future of Yosemite National Park have batted around the idea of banning private automobiles from Yosemite Valley altogether. Currently, no limitations exist, so feel free to drive on approved roads throughout the Park. However, restrictions of some sort are a near certainty in the long term. In the meantime, using the public transportation that is already in place is encouraged whenever possible.

Yosemite Valley Shuttle Bus

While most areas around Yosemite National Park require driving an automobile to the trailhead, there are some options available within Yosemite Valley for those willing to use alternative means of transportation. For many years, a free shuttle-bus system has effectively taken Valley visitors to 19 separate destinations. Although the number of stops is reduced from 19 to 15 during the winter, buses running every 20 minutes still provide service to the most popular places. Hours of operation from mid-November to mid-March are from 9:00 A.M. to 10:00 P.M. A map of the shuttle-bus route is on the back of the *Yosemite Guide*, which is given to visitors entering the Park. The following trailheads described in this book can be accessed by the shuttle bus system:

TRIP	BUS STOP
8. Yosemite Valley West Loop	7. Yosemite Falls
9. Yosemite Valley East Loop	7. Yosemite Falls
10. Yosemite Falls	7. Yosemite Falls
11. Mirror Lake—Tenaya Canyon Loop	19. Lower Pines Campground
12. Little Yosemite Valley	15. Day Use Parking/Curry Village

Badger Pass Bus

Weather permitting, each day free buses take skiers and snowshoers from Yosemite Valley to Badger Pass Ski Area whenever the resort is in operation. Buses leave Curry Village, the Ahwahnee Hotel and Yosemite Lodge daily, and the Wawona Hotel on weekends, at two different times during the morning. Buses depart Badger Pass at two different times in the afternoon for the return trip. Check for specific times at the front desk of the aforementioned accommodations.

Tour Buses

A wide variety of companies run charter buses from various points around Northern California to Yosemite Valley. Check with your travel agent for more information.

Railroads

Amtrak provides service to the town of Merced, from which transportation to Yosemite National Park can be arranged with a number of tour bus companies. Check with your travel agent for more information.

Airports

The nearest major commercial airport is in Fresno, although most people making arrangements to see Yosemite National Park fly into San Francisco International. Rental cars and tour packages can be arranged from both airports. Check with your travel agent for more information.

LODGING

YOSEMITE NATIONAL PARK: From April through October, reservations for lodging in Yosemite are at a premium. Since the number of visitors to the Park is drastically reduced in winter, competition for available space is much less than at busier times of the year. Although calling ahead is always prudent, chances are a room could probably be secured during any non-holiday week without a reservation. As expected, weekends and holiday periods are busier, but with just a modicum of planning finding a place to stay within the park shouldn't be hard. For room reservations at facilities within YNP, call (559) 252-4848 or write Yosemite Reservations, 5410 E. Home Avenue, Fresno, CA 93727. Reservations can be made up to a year and a day before the proposed date of arrival.

While availability is usually not a problem during the winter, don't expect tremendous savings from off-season rates. The cost of a room in the Park is definitely based on location, and even the most Spartan accommodation comes at a premium price. The best bet for an economical place to stay would be to camp in a campground (see Campgrounds below).

Overnight guests have a wide range of options for places to stay within the Park. Beginning at the moderate end of the price spectrum, Yosemite Lodge offers private hotel-style rooms with private bath. In 1998 plans were made to construct some modern lodging facilities to replace the old cabins that were destroyed in the flood of 1997. Curry Village, open only on weekends and holidays during the winter, provides motel style rooms and cabins with a mixture of private and central baths.

At the upper price end, the Ahwahnee and Wawona hotels, both national historic landmarks, pamper guests with old-world charm and exquisite architecture. The Ahwahnee is open year-round, but the Wawona, located outside the Valley near the Mariposa Grove, is open only on weekends and holidays during the winter. All rooms at the Ahwahnee have private bath, while the Wawona has half the rooms with bath and half with central bath.

Other facilities common to summer visitors are closed for the winter season. Housekeeping Camp is closed during the winter

months, and is actually slated for eventual demolition. The High
Sierra Camps along with Tuolumne Meadows and White Wolf lodges
are open in the summer only. However, the recently built Glacier
Point Winter Lodge and the Ski School Hut in Tuolumne Meadows
do provide specialized accommodations for winter recreationists (see
Winter Activities).

Following is a list of lodging facilities open in Yosemite
National Park during the winter:

Facility	Season	Bath	Price	Attractions
Yosemite Lodge	year-round	private	$$-$$$	Yosemite Falls
Curry Village	weekends, holidays	private & central	$$-$$$	Mist Trail
Wawona Hotel	weekends, holidays	private & central	$$$-$$$$	Mariposa Grove
Ahwahnee Hotel	year-round	private	$$$$	Royal Arches

Lodging outside the park is available at a wide variety of locations.
Contact the local chamber of commerce or visitors bureau.

EASTERN SIERRA: Choices for lodging along US 395 at the east
base of the Sierra are limited during the winter. Many motels operate
on a diminished capacity from December through February. Outside
of Mammoth Lakes, which is kept active by the prosperous ski season, many of the smaller towns offer little selection. Call ahead if the
expectation is to find a soft bed and a hot shower.

CAMPGROUNDS

YOSEMITE NATIONAL PARK: Four of the thirteen Yosemite
National Park campgrounds remain open during the winter. In winter all campgrounds are on a first-come, first-served basis. Fees are
charged at all locations. Plenty of space is usually available in all the
campgrounds during the off-season. However, to make reservations
up to 5 months in advance, call (800) 436-7275 or (888) 530-9796 TDD,
between 7 A.M. and 7 P.M. Pacific time, or write to Mail-in
Reservations, NPRS, P.O. Box 1600, Cumberland, MD 21502.

All open campgrounds in the Park have water, flush toilets, picnic tables and fire pits. Sites in Yosemite Valley have bear-proof food storage lockers and are close to laundry and shower facilities. The following is a list of campgrounds open in Yosemite during the winter:

Campground	Daily Fee	Elevation	Location
Upper Pines	$15	4000	Yosemite Valley
Sunnyside Walk-in	$3*	4000	Yosemite Valley
Wawona	$10	4000	Wawona Road (Highway 41)
Hodgdon Meadow	$10	4872	Big Oak Flat Road (Highway 120)

* per person (all other fees are per site)

Additional camping areas are located outside the Park on National Forest lands. Contact the appropriate agency for more information (see Appendix III).

EASTERN SIERRA: All developed campgrounds are closed for the winter on the east side of the central Sierra. However, dispersed camping is allowed on some Forest Service lands. Contact the appropriate Forest Service agency for more information (see Appendix III).

RESTAURANTS

YOSEMITE NATIONAL PARK: For a national park, Yosemite usually has a wide array of dining opportunities, although at a reduced level during the relatively quiet winter months. Plenty of choices still exist for those who do wish to visit the park in the off-season. However, don't expect to find any bargains, as even the cheapest option, the Yosemite Lodge Cafeteria, can be pricey after adding up all of the a la carte selections. Cost aside, in general the quality of the food is good to excellent, the variety wide enough to satisfy most tastes, and the lines, if they exist at all, not long as they typically are in summer.

The following is a list of dining facilities open in Yosemite National Park during winter:

Yosemite Lodge:

Facility	Hours	Days	Price	See Trip
Cafeteria—breakfast	6:30 A.M.-10:30 A.M.	daily	$ - $$	
lunch	11:30 A.M.-2:30 P.M.	daily	$ - $$	
dinner	4:30 P.M.-7:30 P.M.	daily	$ - $$	
Coffee Corner	6:30 A.M.-4:30 P.M.	daily	$	11
Mountain Room—dinner	5:00 P.M.-9:00 P.M.	daily	$$ -$$$	7
Mountain Room Lounge	5:00 P.M.-9:30 P.M.	M-F	$$	9
	noon-10 P.M.	Sat-Sun	$$	9

Yosemite Village:

Degnan's Fast Food	11:00 A.M.-4:00 P.M.	daily	$	10

Ahwahnee Hotel:

Dining Room—breakfast	7:00 A.M.-10:30 A.M.	M-Sat	$$-$$$	8
lunch	11:30 A.M.-2:30 P.M.	M-Sat	$$-$$$	8
dinner *	5:30 P.M.-9:30 P.M.	daily	$$$-$$$$	8
brunch	7:00 A.M.-2:00 P.M.	Sunday	$$$	8
Ahwahnee Bar	noon-9:00 P.M.	daily	$$	

Dinner reservations suggested; dress code

Curry Village:

Pizza	5:00 P.M.-9:00 P.M.	daily	$	12

Wawona Hotel:

Dining Room—breakfast	Call	weekends	$$-$$$	1
lunch	(209) 375-6556	weekends	$$-$$$	1
dinner	for times	weekends	$$$	1

Badger Pass:

Snack Shop	8:30 A.M.-4:30 P.M.	daily	$	4
Lounge	11:00 A.M.-5:00 P.M.	daily	$$	4

Note: all hours are subject to change

EASTERN SIERRA: The east side of the Sierra along US 395 is quite another story. Snowshoers looking for sustenance before or after a trip should lower their expectations from the outset. Most of the tourism that sustains the small towns at the eastern base of the Sierra occurs during the other half of the year that includes fishing season, hunting season, and the height of recreational activities during the summer. Many of the restaurants away from the ski center of Mammoth Lakes close for the season, or at least for a part of the winter. Plan trips carefully, in order to find something to eat along the way to or from the trailhead.

WINTER ACTIVITIES IN YOSEMITE NATIONAL PARK

Snowshoers are blessed with a wide range of choices of how to spend their time while visiting Yosemite. In addition, while snowshoeing may be the chief aim of many when visiting Yosemite, there are plenty of other winter activities to choose from to occupy any free time. Even though many opportunities one would enjoy during the warmer months are not available to winter visitors, there still are plenty of diversions.

Snowshoeing
RANGER TOURS: Besides the trips described in this book, there are other snowshoeing opportunities. Ranger-led 2-hour snowshoe tours occur every day, leaving the Badger Pass Ski Area around mid-morning. A small fee ($2 in '98-99) covers the snowshoe rental. Taking children under 10 is not recommended. The tours are subject to weather and snow conditions, and occur only when Badger Pass Ski Area is operating.
SNOWSHOE RENTALS: The Yosemite Cross-Country Ski Center at Badger Pass rents snowshoes for $11.50 per day. They must be returned by 4 P.M. A Glacier Point Road Winter Trails map is available for 50 cents, showing the network of marked trails originating from Badger Pass.
SNOW CAMPING: Guided trips of one or two nights can be arranged with the Yosemite Cross-Country Ski Center for excursions into the backcountry beyond Badger Pass. Snow travel, survival, and winter camping skills are taught by experts. The $95 per night fee

includes meals and community camping gear. Personal equipment and previous experience are required. Sleeping-bag rentals are available for $10 per day. Call (209) 372-8444 for reservations or more information.

Cross-country Skiing
SKIING: Skating, telemark skiing and cross-country skiing are all available at Badger Pass. Skis, boots and poles can be rented from the Cross-Country Ski Center at half and full day rates ranging from $6.50 to $19.00. The Ski Center opens and closes along with the Badger Pass Ski Area.
SNOW CAMPING: Tours similar to those mentioned above for snowshoers can be arranged for skiers as well.
OVERNIGHT & BACKCOUNTRY TOURS: Guided tours take skiers on overnight trips to the newly constructed Glacier Point Winter Lodge or on multi-day excursions to the Ski School Hut in Tuolumne Meadows. Call the Ski Center for details.

Downhill Skiing & Snowboarding
Badger Pass was the first alpine ski area to be developed in California. Modern-day skiers and boarders can enjoy the 10 runs on the easy-to-moderate slopes below Tempo Dome. The relatively inexpensive prices range from $19.50 for a mid-week half day pass to $28.00 for a full weekend day. Rentals are available at the Badger Pass Ski Lodge. Mid-week guests at Yosemite hotels can ski free the next day (Sunday–Thursday). Badger Pass Ski Area opens when conditions allow and usually runs through Easter weekend.

Ice Skating
The Curry Village Ice Rink is generally open from mid-November to early March, weather permitting. Admission for each session is $5.00 for adults and $4.50 for children, with skate rentals at $2.00. Three 2½ hour sessions are offered on weekdays, with a fourth added on weekend and holiday mornings. Call (209) 372-8341 for more information.

Hiking
When snow is absent from Yosemite Valley, hikers can enjoy a winter

trip to a variety of destinations. Although the Park Service closes the Fourmile Trail to Glacier Point and portions of the Mist and John Muir trails, the other Valley trails remain open during the winter as conditions allow. Check the Visitor Center in Yosemite Village (open daily 9 to 4:30) for more information. The Wilderness Center, which usually provides valuable information and resources for hikers and backpackers, is closed during the winter.

CHAPTER 2

WINTER TRAVEL

WEATHER

Having lived at the east base of the Sierra since 1976, I have seen a number of winters come and go. The one conclusion I have reached regarding the weather is that "normal" is a statistical average that rarely coincides with the real world. During the past twenty-plus years, the weather has run the climatic spectrum, from El Ninos to multi-year droughts, with everything in between. During drought periods, walking the John Muir Trail on bare ground was possible in some winter months, while in other years just reaching the Park was impossible due to the extreme weather.

Despite the scientific advances in weather forecasting, from year to year one does not know what the Sierra winter will be like until the season progresses. However, reliable, short-term weather forecasts are easily available to virtually anyone with a computer, phone or television. A list of appropriate weather forecast sources for the Yosemite region is in Appendix II. The wise recreationist uses available weather information in planning any trip.

Wild variations aside, the climate of the central Sierra can be classified on the whole as dry. The sun shines a great deal of the time. Many an ideal trip occurs during days of bright sunshine following a storm that has blanketed Yosemite with a layer of fresh powder.

16

Most winter storms bringing moisture to the Sierra plow into the range from the west, dropping snow on the higher elevations before moving east across the Great Basin. Typically, storms last no more than a day or two, separated by periods of dry, sunny or partly sunny weather. However, severe storms lasting for days and dropping incredible amounts of snow are not uncommon, particularly as the El Nino winter of '97-'98 has shown. Some days the weather in the Yosemite backcountry is idyllic, some days life-threatening.

Average yearly snowfall is over 60 inches in Yosemite Valley, substantially greater at the higher elevations. Typically, snow falls between November and April, although the heaviest snow comes from December through March. Snowfall has occurred in every month at the upper elevations of the park. Winter temperatures are relatively mild, the average high for the Valley around 55 degrees and the average low near 30 degrees.

The comparatively low elevation of Yosemite Valley does not give an accurate picture of conditions at the higher elevations near the crest of the Sierra. Snowfall is substantially greater in the high country, and temperatures may be as much as 30 degrees colder. This potential for more extreme weather at the upper elevations around Yosemite demands that winter recreationists in this realm should be prepared for the elements.

Average Temperature & Snowfall Charts					
Yosemite Valley (Park Headquarters) 3970'					
	Dec.	Jan.	Feb.	March	April
AVG. HIGH TEMP.	47.4°	47.5°	54.0°	58.3°	65.5°
AVG. LOW TEMP.	27.0°	26.6°	29.2°	31.7°	36.4°
AVG. SNOW DEPTH	2"	4"	4"	2"	0"
AVG. SNOWFALL	10"	18.1"	12.2"	12"	5.8"

Dana Meadows 9800'				
	Dec.	Jan.	Feb.	March	April
AVG. SNOW DEPTH	20"	60"	76"	81"	64"

High & low temperatures & snowfall data not available for this site

Lee Vining 6780'				
	Dec.	Jan.	Feb.	March	April
AVG. HIGH TEMP.	41.2°	40.3°	43.1°	52.0°	59.4°
AVG. LOW TEMP.	20.1°	19.5°	22.0°	28.5°	32.9°
AVG. SNOW DEPTH	0"	3"	4"	1"	0"
AVG. SNOWFALL	9.2"	20.1"	19.1"	6.7"	0.8"

Although firm guarantees are non-existent, sunshine and mild temperatures are a reasonable expectation for a day of snowshoeing in the greater Yosemite region. An average January day in Yosemite Valley has a 39% chance of being sunny and a 74% chance of no precipitation. However, you must be prepared for any condition in the central Sierra—sunshine, snow, sleet, rain, wind and cold all can be extreme at one time or another. Wild variations may even occur during the same day, or even the same hour. Be sure to have the appropriate clothing and equipment to successfully endure whatever conditions might possibly be encountered.

SEASON

The winter snowpack varies greatly from year to year throughout the state of California, making accurate predictions of the optimum time for snowshoeing in the Yosemite area difficult. Compounding this dilemma is the wide range of elevation within the Park boundaries. For instance, snowfall is highly variable at an elevation of 3970 feet in Yosemite Valley, while at 8600 feet in Tuolumne Meadows good snow conditions may be present all the way through June in some years. Typically, there is enough snow above 5,000 feet on the west slope of the central Sierra for decent snowshoeing from December to April. During years of abundant snowfall, the snowshoeing season can be extended considerably, depending on spring temperatures. Since the eastern side of the Sierra lies in the rain shadow of the range, more elevation is usually required for an adequate snowpack, and fluctuations are typically even more variable than on the west side. Obtaining accurate information on current conditions in the Yosemite area is fairly easy via the phone or over the Internet.

Snow conditions around Yosemite will vary, due to a number of different factors. Obviously, altitude is an important determiner of the quantity and quality of the snowpack. After winter storms, when the mercury starts to rise, the snow near the valley floor may be a wet mush or gone altogether, while at Badger Pass, nearly 2,500 feet higher, conditions might be ideal. Geographical location also plays a significant part in snowfall distribution. As Pacific storms hit the Sierra from the ocean, more snow is deposited on the west side of the range than on the east slope. Conditions are also determined by exposure. South-facing slopes are the first to lose their snow, followed by west-, east-, and finally north-facing slopes. Forested areas, protected from the direct rays of the sun, will hang onto their snow longer than open meadows and exposed hillsides. Topography, wind and micro-climates are additional factors influencing the snowpack, making a firm prediction for the season of use a highly variable speculation.

When determining the best time for a particular trip, consider all these factors seriously. Consult the weather, avalanche and ski reports for current conditions before the trip (see Appendix I). Most Forest Service and Park Service ranger stations have useful information as well.

ROUTEFINDING

No backcountry skill is more important in winter than the ability to find your way over snow-covered terrain. There are no trails to follow, at least none built into the soil and maintained by the government, as in the summer. Unless you have the luxury of following a marked trail or the tracks of a previous party, for most of the trips in this book you must be able to interpret major and minor features of the terrain, read a map, and navigate through the backcountry. Space does not allow for a dissertation on the necessary elements of navigation, orientation and routefinding, so you must gather a good understanding of this subject from other sources. The following principles should serve as an outline of a more detailed comprehension of this art.

- *Always study your route carefully before you leave home*
- *Always leave a detailed description of your proposed route with a reliable person*
- *Always carry a topographic map of the area*
- *Always carry a compass*
- *Constantly observe the terrain as you progress*
- *If necessary, mark your trail (and remove your markers on your return)*
- *Always keep your party together as you travel*

A GPS receiver is helpful for determining your position in the backcountry. However, no piece of equipment is an adequate replacement for the skills of navigation, orientation and routefinding.

OBJECTIVE HAZARDS

Sun

For most people, the best days to be snowshoeing in the mountains are days when the snow is fresh and the skies are blue. Unfortunately, these conditions produce their own set of problems: sun, snow and altitude combine to create the perfect reflective oven for baking exposed skin. However, winter usually finds snowshoers fully covered by some sort of apparel, with the exception of the face. Remember to apply an effective sunblock to all exposed areas of skin before venturing out onto snow-covered terrain in the intense winter sun. Reapply the sunblock as necessary throughout the trip.

Snow blindness is a very real problem at these elevations in winter. This malady is caused by prolonged exposure of the eyes to ultraviolet rays. Always wear a pair of goggles or sunglasses that filter out at least 90% of UVA and UVB rays, particularly on clear and sunny days. In addition, side shields on glasses will help to reduce reflective rays.

Dehydration
Becoming dehydrated in the midst of so much frozen liquid may seem ludicrous, but without enough water to replenish reserves, a vigorous activity like snowshoeing can put anyone in danger of just such a problem. Lots of moisture can be lost during strenuous exercise in cold, dry weather simply through respiration. Always carry plenty of water—most streams and lakes are frozen, and eating snow is an inadequate long-term solution.

If open water happens to be found, bear in mind that many water sources in the area are contaminated with pathogens. All water should be treated, even the clearest-looking.

Altitude
The majority of elevations accessible to the casual winter recreationist around the Yosemite area are not considered to be extreme. However, some people, particularly those who live near sea level, may suffer the effects of altitude sickness and its more serious counterpart, acute mountain sickness. Symptoms of altitude sickness include headache, fatigue, loss of appetite, shortness of breath, nausea, vomiting, drowsiness, dizziness, memory loss and loss of mental acuity. Although rare at these elevations, acute mountain sickness is possible. It requires immediate descent and medical attention.

To avoid these maladies, drink plenty of fluids, eat a diet high in carbohydrates prior to and during a trip, and acclimatize slowly. A rapid descent will usually resolve any of the aforementioned symptoms. A severe case of altitude sickness is unlikely at these elevations during one-day trips, although not impossible.

Cold
Hypothermia is a condition in which the body's core temperature drops below normal in response to prolonged exposure to cold. Air temperature is not always the determining factor, as many cases of hypothermia occur when the thermometer registers above freezing. Wind chill, fatigue, and wetness (from rain, melting snow, submersion, or even excessive perspiration) can cause hypothermia.

The best solution for avoiding hypothermia is prevention. Do not get too cold, too tired, or too wet. Dress in layers and take time to

Avalanche run

adjust clothing as conditions change, preventing yourself from becoming too cold as well as preventing excessive wetness, from either precipitation or perspiration. Refrain from pushing on toward exhaustion when tired. Drink plenty of fluids and eat enough energy-producing food. Carry extra clothes in your vehicle to change into after a trip. If you suspect one of your party is experiencing the symptoms of hypothermia, handle the situation immediately. And remember that due to loss of mental acuity, you will not be able to detect symptoms in yourself.

Frostbite, a condition where tissue actually freezes after prolonged exposure to cold, is a potential concern during cold weather. Most susceptible to frostbite are the feet, hands, face and ears. Adequate equipment, including properly fitting footwear, warm socks, gloves and hat, should counteract the prolonged cold that can cause this malady.

Avalanches

Certainly, the most impressive winter hazard in the backcountry is the avalanche. Space does not allow for a complete discussion of avalanches here, and you should read as much as you can about them (see Suggested Reading in Appendix IV: *Mountaineering: The Freedom of the Hills, ABC of Avalanche Safety, Allen & Mike's Really Cool Backcountry Ski Book,* and *Snowshoeing*). Avalanches usually occur due to lack of cohesion between the surface layer and the underlying snow, which can exist for a variety of reasons. They most commonly occur during and soon after storms, and during periods of rising temperatures, but are not limited to these times.

The most avalanche-prone areas include gullies, slopes between 30 and 45 degrees, north-facing slopes in winter, south-facing slopes in spring, lee slopes, treeless slopes, and slopes where younger trees are bordered by more mature forest. In addition, hillsides with a convex slope are prone to avalanche more easily than ones with a concave slope. As much as possible, avoid these areas, particularly during periods of instability.

Even small avalanches pack a considerable wallop. Many years ago after a successful spring climb in the Sawtooth Ridge above Twin Lakes, we decided to glissade down a snow-filled gully for our return route. After a prolonged period of questioning the wisdom of the descent, I dropped to my butt and pushed off down the gully. About halfway down the slope I felt some pressure on my back and instantly started to somersault down the gully. I came to rest at the base of the slope, stripped of my hat, gloves and pack, which were now scattered haphazardly across the snow. My outer parka was halfway over my head and snow filled every available passageway through my remaining clothing. Once I gathered my wits and surveyed the situation, I realized that this tremendous force, which tossed me and my equipment all over the mountain, was created by an avalanche a mere 12 inches high and 6 feet across.

Many people have put forth theories about what to do if caught in an avalanche. My own experience, along with reports from others caught in similar circumstances, has led me to believe that most avalanches occur far too quickly and with too much force for a victim to do much of anything. However, conventional wisdom dictates that you should try to get on your back with your head uphill and make a swimming motion with your arms in an attempt to stay on top of the avalanche, and also—if possible—work your way toward the edge. Good luck.

Although there is no substitute for a wide range of winter experience in determining avalanche risk, there are some guidelines which you would be wise to follow when traveling in the backcountry.

Minimizing Avalanche Danger

- Obtain the current avalanche report for the area (530) 587-2158.
- Select the safest route—follow ridges wherever possible.
- Test slopes for stability. (See Appendix IV for resources on appropriate procedures).
- Travel through suspect terrain quickly, one at a time, from safety zone to safety zone.
- Carry the proper equipment & know how to use it. (Necessary equipment may include shovels, probes, beacons, avalanche cord, cellular phone, first-aid kit).

Cornices

Another impressive feature of the winter landscape is the cornice, an overhanging mass of snow at the crest of a ridge formed where pre-

Cornice

vailing winds drift snowfall leeward over the edge. Cornices pose two problems. Eventually and without warning, cornices will break off and plunge to the slope below, and falling cornices can trigger avalanches on unstable slopes. Obviously, the larger the cornice, the greater the potential for damage. A less obvious danger arises when you're traveling along a ridge: if you snowshoe on the corniced edge of a ridge, you may go for a sudden ride.

TRAIL ETIQUETTE

In general, trail etiquette is much the same in winter as in summer.

◆ *Avoid snowshoeing on existing cross-country ski tracks.* This allows skiers to reuse their tracks for return trips and leaves an existing track for future users.

◆ *Yield the right of way to snowmobiles and cross-country skiers.* Granting the lane to snowmobiles is purely common sense. A person on snowshoes will never win a standoff with a snowmobile. As for skiers, a snowshoer usually has more control over his or her movements than people on skis have.

◆ *Pack out all litter.* Winter, summer, spring or fall, all garbage should be removed from the backcountry.

◆ *Keep pets and their products under control.* If you choose to share the backcountry with your dog, make sure it is a reasonably sociable animal. Chances are you will meet other dogs and other people on the trail, and nothing is more undesirable than having to break up a fight between animals or personally fend off unfriendly canines. Please scatter their droppings as well. Popular trails can become quite unkempt between snowfalls.

SANITATION

Winter presents a whole new situation for dealing with the proper disposal of waste materials. Urinating is fairly straightforward—as long as you don't pee into the snow above a frozen lake or stream. Find a spot well off the trail or a good distance away from your campsite to avoid the resulting visual pollution.

Defecating in the winter backcountry is not nearly as benign. Short of removing the waste altogether, which remains to most of us an undesirable alternative, there is no adequate way that doesn't adversely affect the environment. Burying stool in warmer times of the year allows the waste to gradually decompose and, when a suitable site is chosen, provides minimal risk of groundwater contamination. The danger in winter is that you will select a site where spring thaws cause an excessive amount of poop to find its way into the groundwater or a stream. Some experts speculate that the spread of giardia in the backcountry is due primarily to poor sanitation practices of winter users.

So what should we do? Taking care of your business at home before or after a trip avoids the problem altogether. However, if nature calls at a less convenient time, the best solution is to pack it out. For those who are not blessed with the ability to regulate their stools and have no desire to pack around their own poop, there are a few guidelines to practice. First of all, visual pollution is certainly a concern with site selection—pick a site well away from potential discovery by others. Nothing ruins the winter landscape more quickly than the unfortunate discovery of a previous traveler's waste products staining the snow. Second, choose a location that obviously won't contaminate a water source. Third, find a southern exposure and try to place your results just below the surface. This allows the freeze-thaw cycle to begin breaking down the stool the best way possible, as well as helping to dilute the waste products over the course of the spring melt.

What about used toilet paper? Once again, the best solution is to pack it out. Burning your toilet paper as recommended for backcountry users in other seasons becomes fairly impractical during winter. Carrying out your used paper seems somewhat less obnoxious than packing out the stool, and the minor inconvenience is out-weighed by the greater good.

Although this guide is primarily concerned with day trips, overnight users should be careful when disposing of waste water and any leftover food.

PERMITS

Entrance Fees

All visitors to Yosemite National Park are required to pay for the privilege of entering the Park. In winter, fees are collected at the three western entrances. Be sure to hang onto the receipt, otherwise you will have to pony up the same amount in order to leave. If the particular entrance station happens to be unmanned when you arrive, you will be charged the appropriate fee upon leaving the Park.

Fee Schedule

Type	Cost	Duration	Eligibility
Vehicle	$20	7 Days	
Individual	$10	7 Days	in bus, on foot, horseback, bicycle or motorcycle
Yosemite Pass	$40	1 Year	access to Yosemite only
Golden Eagle Pass	$50	1 Year	access to all national parks
Golden Age Pass	$10	Lifetime	US citizens & permanent residents 62 & over
Golden Access Pass	FREE	Lifetime	blind or permanently disabled citizens or permanent residents of US

Wilderness Permits

Permits are not mandatory for recreationists using the wilderness areas in and around Yosemite National Park for day trips. Overnight users must comply with the regulations described below.

YOSEMITE WILDERNESS: Wilderness permits are required for overnight stays in the backcountry of the Yosemite Wilderness. Permits may be obtained during the winter at the Visitor Center in Yosemite Village or at the Badger Pass Ski Area. Currently, no advance arrangements are necessary for the winter months, as they routinely are for summertime, since numbers are dramatically reduced at this time of year. For more information call (209) 372-0740 or write:

> Wilderness Permits
> P.O. Box 545
> Yosemite, CA 95389

HOOVER WILDERNESS & ANSEL ADAMS WILDERNESS: Overnight users are required to obtain a wilderness permit to enter these wilderness areas on the east side of the Sierra. Quotas are not in effect during the winter, and users can self-register at the appropriate Forest Service ranger station. Advanced reservations can be made by contacting the Forest Service by phone or mail (See Appendix III). Permits are not required for single day use.

CHAPTER 3

EQUIPMENT

SNOWSHOES

The early Seventies saw a significant change in the design and composition of snowshoes. Before this era, the typical snowshoe was constructed of wood and leather. With names like "bearpaw" and "beavertail" describing the classic shapes, outdoorsmen plodded through the snow with altered strides and rangy motions. Most of these predecessors of the modern snowshoe were large and cumbersome. They provided adequate flotation by utilizing a large surface area, which forced users to compensate for their wide and long dimensions by adopting a gait reminiscent of a cowboy walking away from his horse after a long day's ride. In this present era, these old classics are more likely found nailed to the rough-wood paneled walls of a mountain cabin or café than on the backcountry snow. Traditionalists may find a diminishing number of suppliers who still provide old wooden snowshoes for sale.

Taking advantage of modern materials, new designs have revolutionized the manufacture of snowshoes (find a list of suppliers in Appendix III). Lightweight metals, space-age-plastics, and other materials have enabled designers to create lighter, smaller and more efficient snowshoes that are far easier to use. Rather than the cumbersome, oversized snowshoes of old, trim shoes with modern traction devices allow recreationists to pursue their sport with ease over a greater variety of terrain. High-angled slopes that would have been next to impossible for traditional shoes are commonly ascended and descended successfully with the newer equipment. The advanced design of snowshoes has definitely made the winter landscape more accessible by users of all skill levels.

Most modern snowshoes fall into the category known as western, named for their origin in the mountain west. Although some molded models have had recent success, most western snowshoes have a tubular metal frame and some type of synthetic decking. Advanced bindings are attached to the snowshoe at a single flex point, and have traction devices that are well-suited for icy or hard-packed snow conditions.

Snowshoers in the Sierra may meet a wide variety of snow types. Soft, fluffy powder is most often encountered after a storm, with snowfalls of up to 4 feet not uncommon. During these periods, enthusiasts are likely to crave the largest snowshoes they can strap to their feet. Once the snow becomes consolidated, some users to smaller shoes with greater maneuverability. During hard-pack conditions users want the smallest shoe available, with the best traction devices. The spring season presents possibly the greatest challenge, when snow is firm early in the day but turns to wet mush in the afternoon sun.

Manufacturers offer different snowshoes for different types of snow, but most snowshoers will try to get by with a single pair. With prices averaging $200 per pair, owning different sets for a variety of snow conditions may be a luxury. One manufacturer has overcome the cost barrier to owning several pair by making interchangeable tails that can be added to or taken off the main shoe to adapt the length to different snow conditions.

Selecting the best snowshoes for all the possibilities can be daunting. In general, try to get by with the smallest shoe that will reasonably handle the many types of snow encountered in the backcountry. If planning to backpack with snowshoes, you will need a larger size than ones used simply for day trips. For those users who want to climb on steep terrain, a lightweight, smaller shoe with a good traction device is the best choice. If money is no object, buy as many shoes as needed for the variety of situations you will encounter. If it is, make a careful assessment of your needs and buy one or two pairs that will handle most of the situations you expect to find.

Poles

Some people don't use ski poles, but for most snowshoers they provide a nice extra measure of stability. In addition, they provide the upper body with a certain degree of exercise and bear some portion of the load that your legs would otherwise carry alone. Some poles can be threaded together when their baskets are removed, thereby doubling as avalanche probes.

CLOTHING

The backcountry rule for clothing is summed up in one word—layering. Many layers of lightweight clothing allow greater flexibility to adapt to the changing conditions of strenuous exercise in winter. Adding or subtracting a layer or two allows the backcountry user to regulate his or her body temperature more easily than a few thick layers of clothing would.

Underwear

Many synthetic materials have been developed for use in the backcountry. Select ones that will conduct perspiration to your outer layers of clothing quickly while maintaining warmth. As nice as cotton feels against your skin, once it gets wet, you get cold.

Pants

Choose pants made from synthetic materials or wool that are lightweight, loose-fitting, water-resistant and durable. A pair of nylon shell pants over your regular pants will help to shed snow and protect your legs from wind. Gore-Tex or an equivalent material will help keep you dry in wet conditions.

Torso

Modern fabrics have greatly aided in keeping recreationists warm and dry. As stated, multiple layers allow you to adjust to changing conditions whether they be external or internal fluctuations in temperature. With the advent of pile, fleece and other synthetic products, the snowshoer has a wide range of choices for what to wear around the upper body next to the primary layer of underwear. Shirts, vests, pullovers and jackets can all be used alone or in combination to achieve comfort. Down-filled vests and jackets are still popular choices for warmth, light weight, and compressibility—just make sure they don't get wet. Your outer layer should be a waterproof or water-resistant parka with a hood that will protect you from wind and weather.

Hats

In the Sierra a hat should protect you from the intense rays of the sun on those idyllic, clear days. When it's cold you will need one to keep your head warm. A "stocking hat" that can adjust to protect your face also during extreme conditions is an excellent choice.

Gloves/Mitts

Next to cold feet, cold hands can make you nearly as miserable in the backcountry. Mitts will keep your hands warmer than gloves. Usually the best combination for handwear is an inner liner of synthetic material or wool and an outer shell of waterproof nylon reinforced in critical areas.

Boots

Protecting your feet from the cold temperatures and wet conditions of winter is of the utmost importance. Many snowshoe trips, starting out as pleasant excursions into winter wonderlands, have turned into living nightmares due to agonizingly wet and bitterly cold feet. Not too long ago there weren't many options for footwear in the snowshoeing world. Whatever hiking boots you used during summer were the same ones you would strap into your snowshoes in winter, properly coated with multiple applications of some waxy sealant in a less-than-totally-effective attempt to keep your feet dry. Nowadays, a number of companies are producing winter-type boots suitable for many outdoor pursuits, some more appropriate for snowshoeing than others.

Winterizing one's summer boots is still an option that many continue to pursue, and one that is quite effective in spring. If choosing this option, make sure the footwear is substantial enough to provide adequate support and comfort when attached to a pair of snowshoes. Fortunately, the Yosemite area does not see the number of bitterly cold days that some regions suffer, but nevertheless your boots must provide a moderate level of warmth. In addition sufficiently protecting boots from wetness is a must, particularly in spring, when warm days begin to turn the snowpack into a wet mush. Consult your local backcountry retailer for the best water-protection product for your particular type of boot.

If you decide to use winter boots, select a pair that will provide the necessary rigidity required for successful operation of your snowshoes. Many winter boots are designed for walking around in the snow, but are not necessarily made for snowshoeing. Some models come with felt liners for extra protection from the cold; make sure if you purchase a pair that these boots fit with and without the liners. Talk to an informed clerk at a reliable outdoor store for their recommendations.

Gaiters

A good pair of gaiters is a winter essential for keeping snow out of your boots. Select gaiters that are made from durable fabrics and are easy to put on and remove.

Socks

Socks are probably the most important piece of clothing when it comes to keeping you warm. There seem to be as many sock combinations as there are backcountry users, so pick a mix that works best for you. Select liners of synthetic fabrics that will pass moisture easily to the outer socks. Outer socks should be thicker wool or synthetic blends which can keep your feet warm even when wet.

SAFETY DEVICES

Avalanche Beacons

If you expect to travel extensively through potential avalanche terrain, a set of avalanche beacons is a wise choice. To be effective, everyone in your party must carry a device and be trained in its use. Batteries should always be checked prior to your departure.

Avalanche Cord

A less expensive alternative to beacons, avalanche cord is a thin cord, 100 feet or so in length, that snowshoers secure to their bodies spaced at equal intervals. In the event of an avalanche, rescuers can follow an exposed section of cord to the victim.

Avalanche Probes

Probes aid in finding a buried victim. The most efficient way to carry avalanche probes is to have ski poles that will connect into a single probe. Teammates can pierce the snowpack with the probes in search of victims.

Snow Shovels

Everyone in your party should carry a lightweight snow shovel. Not only essential in avalanche rescue, snow shovels are of immense help if a temporary shelter has to be constructed.

Cellular Phones

Technology has produced many wonderful gadgets designed to make our lives easier, although I am not sure that statement applies to cellular phones. Personal pet peeves aside, cellular phones do provide an instant link with the outside world in case of an emergency. As long they are not abused, cellular phones can be a tremendous resource in times of real trouble.

NAVIGATIONAL AIDS

Obviously, as snowcover is the most significant distinction of Yosemite in winter when compared to the summer landscape. While hikers and backpackers, without much thought, typically follow a well-defined trail to their favorite destination during summer, winter travelers are governed by a much different set of rules. In the absence of the established trails of summer, a modicum of navigational skill is necessary to safely negotiate the snow-covered backcountry. Most trail signs and blazes on trees are lost, and even dominant physical features, such as streams and lakes, can disappear or be significantly altered by a normal snowpack. In order to successfully negotiate the winter landscape, you must have certain equipment and a sufficient knowledge of its use.

GPS Systems
With the advent of access to the GPS system by the general public, many outdoor lovers have come to depend upon hand-held monitors for accurately locating their position in the backcountry. Particularly in winter, when trails and landmarks become obscured by the deepening snows, GPS devices can be a great asset, although certainly not an absolute necessity. In densely forested terrain or during inclement weather, the GPS can save you from confused wandering, which could lead to much more severe consequences. However, a GPS device is no substitute for backcountry savvy and the knowledge of how to read the landscape coupled with the ability to use a map and compass.

Map & Compass
When traveling through mountain snows, a USGS 7 ½ minute topographic map is an essential element for your pack, especially when journeying along unmarked routes. Typically, these maps provide detailed topographic information, including contours, elevations of important landmarks, and the location of physical features such as streams, lakes, peaks, and canyons. As with many tools, these maps are next to useless without an understanding of them. If you presently lack the ability to use these maps, you may be able to gain it through programs of local outdoor groups, through adult education courses, or by consulting an appropriate publication.

In addition to these USGS maps, a number of other maps cover the Yosemite region. The Forest Service provides maps of its districts, but they lack contour lines and are at too small a scale to be useful for backcountry travel. Numerous recreation maps are published by private companies, but they also lack the necessary scale for finding your way in the wild. There is no good substitute for the USGS maps.

A map covering the area of your travel is a necessary item, but is incomplete without a properly working compass. Poor visibility due to weather or terrain can disorient backcountry users, and a compass is the best way to regain one's bearings. Avoid cheap models— a flawed compass is worse than none at all.

MAPS

A maps is provided for each trip in this book, produced from reduced copies of 7 ½-minute USGS quadrangles. The first number following the "Map" heading in a trip description refers to the book's map for that route.

Topographic Maps
Many outdoor retailers carry USGS maps. Below is a listing of these maps for the greater Yosemite region with corresponding snowshoe trip numbers.

USGS Map Name	Trip Numbers
1. Pickel Meadow	39, 40, 41
2. Fales Hot Springs	no trips
3. Mt. Jackson	38
4. Buckeye Ridge	36, 37
5. Twin Lakes	34, 35, 37, 38
6. Matterhorn Peak	37
7. Dunderberg Peak	30, 31, 32, 33, 35
8. Lundy	30, 31, 32, 33
9. Falls Ridge	23
10. Tioga Pass	23
11. Mt. Dana	25, 26, 27, 28, 29
12. Lee Vining	26
13. Ackerson Mountain	16, 18, 19, 20, 21, 22, 23
14. Tamarack Flat	23
15. Yosemite Falls	9, 10, 11, 23

Index of USGS Maps

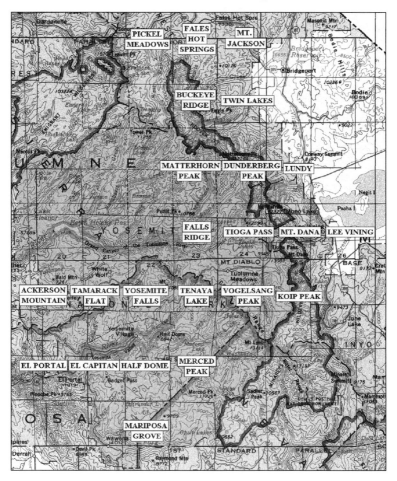

The United States Geological Survey produces the 7 ½ minute quadrangles, generally regarded as the finest maps available to the general public. State indexes can be ordered from the government at (800)
USA-MAPS or (800) HELP-MAP, or by writing to:

USGS Information Services
Box 25286
Denver, CO 80225

With the appropriate state and map names, you can order directly
from the Customer Service department of the USGS at (800) 435-7627
(or online at usgs.gov). In 1999, maps were selling for $4.00 a piece,
plus a small shipping and handling charge per order. The USGS
accepts VISA or MasterCard for payment.

Computer Software

Software companies have developed computer programs utilizing
the USGS maps as a base. Some of these programs are better than others, having a variety of options you can use to customize maps for
personal use. With a decent desktop color printer, you can produce
maps at home that rival the quality of the USGS ones, albeit not on
the same-size sheet of paper. The cost of a typical program is around
the cost of 10 to 15 maps, which makes the price of the software reasonable if you plan on purchasing many maps. Your local backpack-
ing store is usually the best source for these programs. Sometime in
the future we may be able to buy computer disks directly from the
USGS containing a specified number and selection of topo maps.

Forest Service Maps

The US Forest Service produces a number of good maps that are well-
suited for general purposes for areas around Yosemite but, as a rule,
should not be substituted for the more accurate USGS maps. These
small-scale maps are often helpful in determining highway routes to
trailheads and for gaining a wider perspective of the territory. They
can be purchased at the appropriate Forest Service Ranger Station
(see Appendix II). A list of maps covering the greater Yosemite area
with a brief description of each follows:

◆ *Inyo National Forest*—a ½" = 1 mile map covering lands east of Yosemite National Park from Mono Lake southward.

◆ *Sierra National Forest*—a ½" = 1 mile map covering lands south of Yosemite National Park to Fresno.

◆ *Toiyabe National Forest*—a ½" = 1 mile map covering lands east of Yosemite National Park from Sonora Pass northward.

◆ *Hoover Wilderness*—a 1" = 1 mile map with contours covering the Hoover Wilderness and a large section of northeast Yosemite.

Park Service Maps

The Park Service provides a fine array of maps for a variety of recreational purposes that may be purchased at the Visitor Center in Yosemite Valley. The Winter Trails maps are of particular interest for snowshoers and are relatively inexpensive at 50 cents apiece. They can be obtained at the Visitor Center and the Village Store in Yosemite Valley, the service stations at Crane Flat and Wawona, and most of the time at the trailheads.

◆ *Crane Flat Winter Trails*—a ½" = 1 mile map printed on brown paper showing the marked trails in the vicinity of Crane Flat.

◆ *Glacier Point Road Winter Trails*—with an approximate scale of 1" = 1 mile, this map printed on blue paper shows the marked trails radiating from the Badger Pass Ski Area, including the 10-mile route to Glacier Point.

◆ *Mariposa Grove Winter Trails*—this large-scale map, printed on green paper, shows the marked trails of the Mariposa Grove of Giant Sequoias.

Additional Maps

Private-sector maps of Yosemite have been produced by a handful of concerns. Two recommended maps are:

◆ *Topographic Map of Yosemite Valley*—a 1:24,000 scale map printed on waterproof plastic material covering the valley from the Merced Gorge to Tenaya Canyon and Little Yosemite Valley. This map is an excellent accompaniment for Trips 9-15. Published by Wilderness Press. $6.95.

◆ *Topographic Map of Yosemite National Park and Vicinity*—a 1:125000 scale map printed on waterproof plastic material showing the entire Park and surrounding backcountry areas. Published by Wilderness Press. $6.95.

A plethora of other maps have been created for Yosemite National Park—you could go broke trying to accumulate them all. However, the maps above should be more than adequate to provide the information you need.

EQUIPMENT CHECKLIST

GEAR:
Snowshoes
Ski poles/avalanche probes
Pack
10 essentials:
    maps
    compass
    flashlight or headlamp (extra batteries & bulb)
    knife
    extra food
    extra clothing
    sunglasses & sunscreen
    matches (in waterproof container)
    candles (or firestarter)
    first aid/emergency kit
Toilet paper
Repair kit: cord, tape, safety pins, etc.

Water bottles or thermos
Signalling devices: whistle & mirror
Safety equipment:
 avalanche cord
 avalanche detectors
Snow shovel

OPTIONAL GEAR:
Camera
Binoculars
GPS receiver
Cellular phone

CLOTHING:
Winter boots
Gaiters
Socks (liners & outer socks)
Shell parka (Gore-Tex or equivalent)
Shell pants (Gore-Tex or equivalent)
Jacket
Vest
Shirt
Gloves or mitts
Hats (for sun & cold)
Underwear
Pants

Snowshoeing equipment

CHAPTER 4

HOW TO USE THIS GUIDE

This guidebook is designed specifically for snowshoers who want to go on one-day trips in the central Sierra, principally by western access into Yosemite National Park and from U.S. Highway 395 on the east side of the range. Twenty-one of the book's forty-one trips are in Yosemite, while the remainder are found on the eastern fringe of the Sierra, between Mammoth Lakes to the south and Highway 108 (Sonora Pass road) to the north. I have tried to not simply to tailor existing cross-country ski routes for snowshoe trips, but to identify areas that are specifically well-suited for snowshoeing, although some trips will indeed correspond to known cross-country routes.

Just over half of the trips described are classified as suited for snowshoers of moderate abilities, 24% for beginners and 24% for the more experienced. These ratings are both subjective and liable to the vagaries of nature. A trip rated difficult can easily be accomplished on a day when the weather is clear and the snow conditions perfect, while a half-mile trip rated as easy can turn into a desperate struggle for snowshoers wading through 5 feet of fresh powder while a driving wind knocks them to and fro.

My intention was to provide enough information to direct readers to the trailhead, to a destination, and back again—but not so much as to require lots of reading time on the trail.

Duration: This information is my subjective evaluation of how much of a typical winter's day should be required for the complete enjoyment of a particular trip. Surely, there will be those who can complete trips in less time than is listed, just as others may feel hurried. Hopefully, the average snowshoer will find these estimates reasonable.

Distance: Distances have been accurately determined in the field using the 7.5' USGS quadrangles. Since exact routes are difficult to duplicate on the ever-changing winter landscape, there may be some slight variations in distance covered, but certainly nothing dramatic. When the total distance depends on how much of a road is plowed, that is noted.

Difficulty: For the purpose of this guide, difficulty ratings have been grouped into four categories: easy, moderate, difficult and extreme. Easy trips should be well-suited to beginning snowshoers as the terrain is gentle, the trips are relatively short, and the routefinding is minimal. Moderate trips pass over more complex terrain, are typically longer, and require some routefinding skills to successfully negotiate. Trips that receive a difficult rating move the snowshoer across steeper terrain, cover greater distances and may necessitate considerable routefinding skill. These journeys may present more objective dangers as well, such as avalanche potential or a greater possibility of exposure to inclement weather. The last rating, extreme, is for those trips that push the limits of technical skill, endurance and vulnerability to the forces of nature. These journeys are for experienced snowshoers who are technically proficient, in good condition, and well qualified to evaluate potential hazards.

Elevation: The first four-digit entry under this heading is for the trailhead elevation at the start of a trip. The second number is the elevation at the high point of a round trip, except in cases where the destination is substantially lower than the highest point en route. For these trips, three elevations are listed, the third being the destination. For the few one-way trips that require a shuttle, three elevations are listed: the beginning trailhead, the high point, and the ending trailhead.

Maps: Here you will find the number of the map in the book and the names of the corresponding 7.5′ quadrangles covering the trip.

Introduction: The introduction gives a brief picture of the highlights of the journey.

How to get there: Clear instructions are given for getting to the trailhead.

Description: The trip description gives complete directions for the route. Still, the intent is to avoid an overly detailed discourse so that you can enjoy the backcountry experience without continual dependence on a book.

FYI: Under the "For Your Information" heading, are additional matters of importance.

Warm-ups: Many winter enthusiasts find a trip to the winter backcountry incomplete unless they sit by the fire sipping their favorite brew after an exhilarating romp through the snow. Those who enjoy a hot drink or a warm meal following a snowshoe trip, will find some suggestions here. A completely subjective and random formula was used in evaluating these establishments. They had to in some way capture certain undefinable elements related to an outdoor ambiance, as well as provide decent food or drink at a reasonable cost. Other intangibles were considered, not the least of which was whether the staff was reasonably friendly to poorly dressed, unshaven, perspiration-soaked, snow-sodden customers.

CHAPTER 5

YOSEMITE NATIONAL PARK

Yosemite is certainly one of the most visited parks in the National Park system. At peak times during the summer, prospective visitors are turned away when the Park reaches a predetermined level of tourists which in some administrator's mind represents an unacceptable level of overcrowding. Such overwhelming affection for the area has earned Yosemite the reputation of being a "Disneyland in the mountains." Between Memorial Day and Labor Day weekends, there are times when Yosemite Valley seems to be nothing more than a forested megalopolis with incredible scenery. However, winter can produce a different effect.

As the thermometer begins to register colder temperatures and a blanket of snow covers the high country, the hustle and bustle of Yosemite's busy season is soon forgotten. The number of tourists steadily declines as the pleasant Indian summers segues into the mild days of late autumn, finally giving way to the cooler and shorter days of early winter. Those hearty souls willing to experience the Park from December through March find tranquillity and serenity amid the extraordinary surroundings. A whole new range of possibilities opens up for snowshoers and cross-country skiers willing to take advantage of Yosemite's forgotten season.

While three major state highways provide access to Yosemite from the western valleys of California, three major areas of winter trails furnish recreationists with plenty of options for pursuing their pastimes in the snow. Along the Wawona Road just inside the Park's South Entrance, the Mariposa Grove of Giant Sequoias tempts snowshoers with a number of trails winding through the massive trees. Snowshoers can experience the awe and wonder of the giant sequoias on trips to the Upper and Lower Mariposa groves.

Badger Pass, five miles up the Glacier Point Road from the junction with the Wawona Road at Chinquapin, is Yosemite's premier winter recreation area. Opening in 1935, Badger Pass became the nation's first downhill ski resort. As interest in winter sports has widened over the years, Badger Pass has expanded its range of activities to meet the changing demand. Along with traditional alpine skiing, the resort now welcomes snowboarders and telemarkers to the slopes below Tempo Dome. The Cross-Country Ski Center caters not only to cross-country skiers, but to skaters and backcountry skiers as well. With the increased popularity of snowshoeing, the Ski Center rents snowshoes and provides Ranger-led snowshoe tours and guided overnight trips. From Badger Pass a number of marked trails lure both beginner and advanced skiers and snowshoers alike. Famous views abound from destinations such as Glacier Point, Sentinel Dome and Dewey Point. Away from the marked trails, the backcountry beckons more adventurous winter travelers to make their own tracks into the hinterlands.

Near the junction between the Big Oak Flat and Tioga roads, Crane Flat welcomes a wide cross-section of winter enthusiasts to the gentle terrain found around the point where the Tioga Road is closed for the season. Beginners can sample a number of short, marked trails crisscrossing the meadows of Crane Flat, as they gain experience with the techniques and equipment of a new sport. Moderately experienced snowshoers can tackle a variety of lengthier trails, some marked and some unmarked, leading through forested terrain to viewpoints or additional meadows. The snowcovered Tioga Road offers more experienced travelers a gateway into the Yosemite back-country and exciting opportunities for multi-day trips.

While the Mariposa Grove, Badger Pass and Crane Flat regions offer reliable snow conditions in all but the driest of winters, trails originating from Yosemite Valley present additional chances to experience areas of the Park on snowshoes. Although adequate snowcover is a sporadic occurrence in the Valley, enough snow can be found at various times to create a most enjoyable snowshoe experience. In addition, although some of the trails beginning at the Valley floor may be snow free at certain times during the winter, plenty of snow will soon appear as elevation is gained on those trails that climb out of the Valley. As with winter trails from Badger Pass and Crane Flat, routes from Yosemite Valley provide additional opportunities for multi-day trips into the heart of the backcountry.

The winter trails in Yosemite have long been popular with the ski crowd. Only recently have snowshoers started to enjoy these trails in significant numbers. Therefore, plan on sharing your paths with cross-country skiers, especially around Badger Pass and Crane Flat. Observe proper winter trail etiquette at all times (see Chapter 2). Park regulations prohibit taking pets onto the trails.

Services in the Park are significantly reduced during the winter. Service stations at Crane Flat and Wawona are open only during daylight hours, but gas can be purchased 24 hours with a debit or credit card. Stores in Yosemite Village, Yosemite Lodge and Wawona remain open during winter, but typically close by early evening. Accommodations and dining vary according to location (see Lodging & Restaurants, Chapter 1).

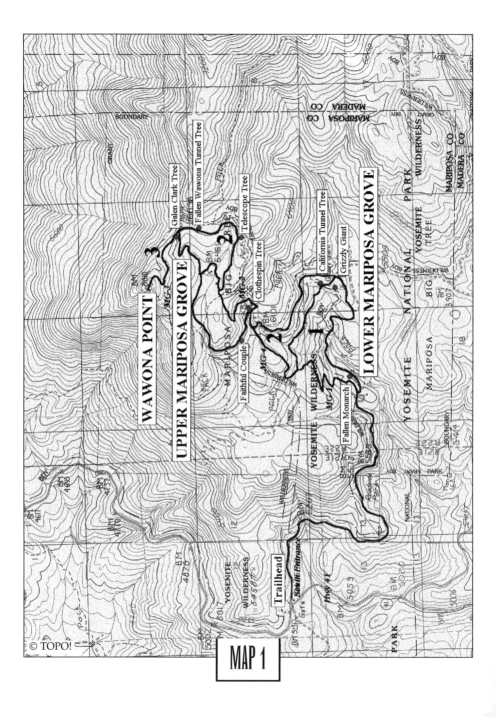

MAP 1

MARIPOSA GROVE
LOWER LOOP

Duration: ½ day
Distance: 2 ¼ mile loop + 4 mile round trip walk or snowshoe
Difficulty: Easy
Elevation: 5150/5980
Maps: 1; *Mariposa Grove* 7.5' quadrangle, 1990
     Mariposa Grove Winter Trails

Introduction: Any Yosemite experience is incomplete without a trip through one of the Park's three groves of giant sequoias. The Mariposa Grove is the largest, and has the oldest giant sequoia in the park, the Grizzly Giant. At the height of tourist season, from May through October, Mariposa is also the most visited grove, when trams carry sightseers up the 2-mile access road to the visitor center and beyond. Without this easy access, winter enthusiasts can enjoy the grove in peace and quiet, when a fresh blanket of snow carpets the ground and gracefully clings to the branches.

The price of experiencing the sequoias in such seclusion is having to walk or snowshoe those first two miles up to the lower grove. Once there, snowshoers can choose from a variety of different routes that weave through the grove. Routes are marked and easy to follow, although they all involve a steady climb. The following trip is the shortest of the three in this guide, leading you to many of the grove's most famous landmarks, including the Grizzly Giant, Tunnel Tree and Fallen Monarch.

Trailhead: Near the south entrance of Yosemite, approximately 60 miles north of Fresno. Just past the entrance station, where Highway 41 bends west, find the ample parking area for Mariposa Grove.

Description: The first part of the trip is either a hike or a snowshoe along the 2-mile access road to Mariposa Grove. The Park Service usually has one side of the road plowed from the parking lot up to the beginning of the lower grove, giving you the option of snowshoeing the snow-covered side or walking on the pavement. Whichever way you choose, follow the road as it climbs and winds through light-to-moderate forest. Pass a restroom and picnic area at the 1 ¼-mile mark and continue to steadily climb. Two miles from the parking lot, you begin a short descent near a curve in the road and reach the signed entrance to the Mariposa Grove. The rest of the road remains unplowed during winter.

At the end of the access-road loop, is a winter information area signboard where a *Mariposa Grove Winter Trails* map can be purchased for 50 cents. Rather than continue up the snow-covered road straight ahead, follow the loop a short distance around to the start of the MG-1 Trail. The wide path is delineated by rectangular yellow markers attached to trees. Climb straight up through moderate forest until the first giant sequoia appears, after which the path makes a winding ascent through the trees. A half mile from the trailhead you reach a signed three-way junction with the MG-4 Trail.

At the junction, bear right (east) remaining on MG-1 and following the signed directions for GRIZZLY GIANT 0.5. Descend briefly before you resume the climb, still through moderate forest. Where the track narrows, you begin a mild descent down to a small creek. Beyond the creek, you make a quick climb up to an area where you will find the California Tunnel Tree.

Because access to the famed Wawona Tunnel Tree in the upper grove was blocked by snowfall during the winter months, the California Tunnel Tree was carved in 1881, allowing visitors year-round passage through the large hole at the base. When the original tree succumbed to the elements during the winter of 1968-69, the California Tunnel Tree became the only "Tunnel Tree" left standing in the park. While hordes of summer tourists flock to this site to have their photographs taken while standing in the "tunnel," chances are very good that you won't have to wait in line for a similar experience in the winter months.

Leaving the California Tunnel Tree behind, climb up the hillside toward the main road, finding the Grizzly Giant down a short path near the top of the hill to your right. As you stand gazing at the sheer enormity of this tree, you realize that this giant of giant sequoias is aptly named.

Now leave MG-1 and turn down the snow-covered main road, heading back toward the visitor center on a moderate descent. Follow the road as it winds around, and ½ mile from the junction you encounter the Bachelor Tree and the Three Graces. Continue down the road, passing more sequoias along the way. Just before the end of the route, you encounter the Fallen Monarch reposing alongside the road. The downed tree gives you a more complete perspective of the sheer enormity of these giant sequoias as you walk alongside this tree for a considerable stretch, its girth rising high overhead.

A short distance beyond the Fallen Monarch, you reach the visitor center, thereby closing your 2 ¼-mile snowshoe loop. From here you must still hike or snowshoe the remaining 2 miles back to the parking lot.

FYI: For a more extensive trip through the Mariposa Grove, see Trips 2 and 3.

Warm-ups: The old world Victorian elegance of the dining room at the Wawona Hotel is a pleasant complement to the more stately majesty of the Ahwahnee dining room. However, a marked difference is the casual dress code at Wawona, allowing merely semi-respectable snowshoers the opportunity to enjoy an excellent meal. The selection of entrees is somewhat reduced from the regular-season menu, but the presentation and the ambiance more than compensate for the sparse selection. Prices are moderate to moderately expensive. If you're looking for a buffet or a bargain, head back toward Fresno.

The Wawona Hotel has reduced hours in winter. The dining room was open from lunch on Thursday through Sunday brunch during the winter of '98-'99. Contact Yosemite Reservations or (209) 375-6556 for more information about the restaurant hours or about lodging.

MARIPOSA GROVE
UPPER LOOP

Duration: Full day
Distance: 6 mile loop + 4 mile round trip walk/snowshoe
Difficulty: Moderate
Elevation: 5150/6640
Maps: 1; *Mariposa Grove* 7.5' quadrangle, 1990
　　　　Mariposa Grove Winter Trails

Introduction: A trip through the giant sequoias is one of the musts for any visit to Yosemite. The graceful touch of fresh snow adds a serene ambiance to the awesome grandeur of these immense and ancient trees. The Mariposa Grove is the largest and most popular of the three groves in the Park, but much less visited in winter. Snowshoers can experience the majesty of the big trees without the hordes of tourists common to the summer experience.

Even more big trees will be found on this trip than on Trip 1, including curiosities such as the original Wawona Tunnel Tree (although it did topple in 1969), the Telescope and Clothespin trees, and the Faithful Couple. The Galen Clark, Mariposa and Columbia trees are other major sequoias in the upper grove. Although the lower grove is quite impressive, more sequoias will be seen in the upper grove. By following this route the notable giants of the lower grove, as seen in Trip 1, won't be missed as you will pass all those major attractions as well.

For the most part, the description below follows the marked snow trails on the way up to the upper grove and then descends via the main road, thereby minimizing the amount of backtracking. Remember, you will have to hike or snowshoe the first 2 miles up to the trailhead at the beginning of the lower grove, just as described in Trip 1.

Trailhead: Follow directions in Trip 1 to the Mariposa Grove parking lot.

Description: Follow directions in Trip 1 to the junction between the MG-1 and MG-4 Trails. From the junction, follow the MG-4 Trail as it climbs north-northwest and then winds around until it assumes a north-northeast bearing. After 0.4 mile you connect into the main Mariposa Grove road curving east. Head up the road for about 0.1 mile, to where the road curves back around to the west. Here you will find the next trail segment, MG-2, beginning near the Clothespin Tree, a giant sequoia with a thin gap at the base. You climb moderately along MG-2, quickly following a horseshoe bend in the trail. Continue the moderate ascent until the grade eases near the crest of a hill, where the forest momentarily becomes more open, until the route switchbacks and heads back into medium forest cover. You reach the main road once more, completing the ½ mile MG-2 Trail.

At this junction, bear left and follow the road as it curves around, passing a restroom building and then the Mariposa Grove Museum. Having reached the upper grove, you can't help but notice the increased number of giant sequoias scattered around the area. After ¼ mile you reach the loop road junction, where you should bear to the right (west). You continue to climb up the road for another ¾ mile, reaching the Galen Clark Tree and a junction with the MG-3 Trail to Wawona Point (see Trip 3). Galen Clark, who came to the mountains because of ill health but eventually lived another 53 years, discovered the Mariposa Grove and was the first guardian of Yosemite State Park.

Another 0.1 mile of ascent leads you to the high point of the route near the Fallen Wawona Tunnel Tree, which greeted tourists from 1881 until 1969, when it succumbed to the forces of nature during a particularly harsh winter. The road now begins a gentle descent, and you reach the Telescope Tree in another ½ mile. Stand in the base of the tree and look up through its length to the sky. Back on the road, a ¼-mile journey returns you to the junction with the road and MG-2, 3 ¼ mile from the trailhead. If the shortest way back is preferred, follow your original route back to the visitor center. But by following the description below, you can vary your return route, taking the road back to the trailhead.

Retrace your steps for ¼ mile past the museum to the road junction. This time head downhill to your left (west) and follow the road on a long arc around a hill. Along the way you will pass a number of sequoias, including the very thick Mariposa Tree. After ¾ mile the road bends sharply near the Clothespin Tree and you follow your original steps for another 0.1 mile to the junction with MG-4.

From the MG-4 junction, you continue to follow the main road as it descends for ¾ mile to a junction with MG-1 near the California Tunnel Tree and the Grizzly Giant. Along the way you pass the Faithful Couple, a pair of sequoias joined at the base but separating near the top.

The remaining mile of road makes a winding descent across a number of small creeks, passing through the lower grove. Along the

Mariposa Grove Museum

way, you will see the Bachelor and the Three Graces, as well as the Fallen Monarch. When you reach the visitor center you have completed the 6-mile loop, but still have another 2-mile hike or snowshoe back to the parking lot.

FYI: If you wish to stay overnight in the Mariposa Grove, Park regulations mandate that you camp above the Clothespin Tree. Camping in this area is allowed between December 1st and April 15th. Overnight users must secure a wilderness permit from the Badger Pass Ski Area or the Valley visitor center.

Warm-ups: See Trip 1.

WAWONA POINT

Duration: Full day
Distance: 7 miles round trip + 4-mile round-trip walk/snowshoe
Difficulty: Moderate to difficult
Elevation: 5150/6810
Maps: 1; *Mariposa Grove* 7.5' quadrangle, 1990
       Mariposa Grove Winter Trails

Introduction: The best way to top off a trip to the upper Mariposa Grove is to make the ½ mile climb along an abandoned road to the vista at Wawona Point. The route leaves the Mariposa road at the Galen Clark Tree and makes a moderate ascent up to the 6810-foot summit of Wawona Point. From there, you have fine views of the surrounding countryside and, on clear days, a vista across the San Joaquin Valley to the Coast Range hills.

Trailhead: Follow directions in Trip 1 to the Mariposa Grove parking lot.

Description: Follow directions in Trip 2 to the junction between the main road through Mariposa Grove and the MG-3 Trail.

From the junction near the Galen Clark Tree, follow the path of the old road on a continuous moderate ascent through medium forest cover of mostly pine with some fir. One-third mile from the junction, you follow the road around a switchback. Continue to climb until you reach a large flat at the top of the hill. Head to the edge of the flat for some fine views of the Wawona Basin and, on clear days, the Coast Range across the San Joaquin Valley.

FYI: Be sure to start early enough to get all the way up to the viewpoint and back to the parking lot. When the snow is fresh, breaking trail all the way from the visitor center to Wawona Point can be taxing.

Warm-ups: See Trip 1.

View from Wawona Point

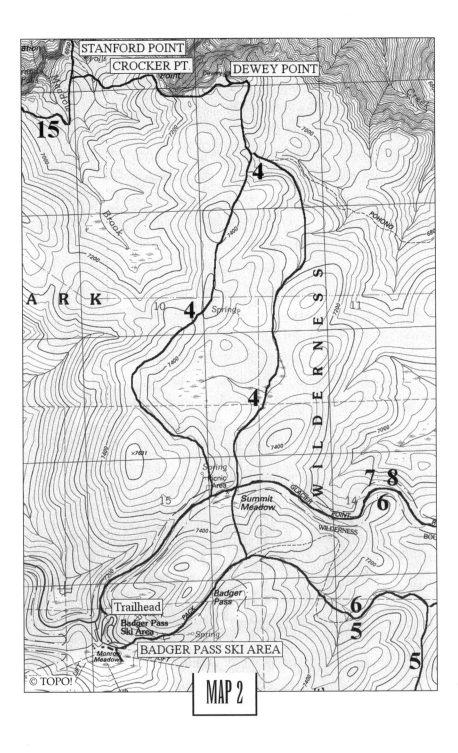

MAP 2

DEWEY POINT
RIDGE TRAIL—MEADOW TRAIL LOOP

Duration: ¾ day
Distance: 7 mile loop trip
Difficulty: Moderate
Elevation: 7180/7450/7385
Maps: 2; *El Capitan* 7.5' quadrangle, 1990
      Glacier Point Road Winter Trails

Introduction: Dewey Point may well be the most popular winter destination for outdoor recreationists in the Park. A sunny weekend day will see hundreds of skiers and snowshoers being drawn to the edge of the cliff. However, crowds should not deter you from the experience of gazing across the deep cleft of Yosemite Valley to the imposing sheer granite face of El Capitan. Other Yosemite landmarks visible from the point are almost too numerous to count, including many of the high peaks in the center of and on the eastern edge of the Park.

    Two marked routes head toward the vista at Dewey Point, Ridge Trail #14 and Meadow Trail #18. By far the less physically taxing is the Meadow Trail, as the grade is extremely gentle from the Glacier Point Road to the junction where the two trails meet. This is the route most cross-country skiers use. By comparison, the Ridge Trail rolls up and down like a drunken sailor on a stormy sea. Still, by snowshoeing standards the Ridge Trail is a reasonably pleasant route. For variety, this trip follows the Ridge Trail to Dewey Point and returns via the Meadow Trail. Finally, rather than return from the end of the Meadow Trail along the Glacier Point Road, you can climb up to the old Glacier Point Road near Badger Pass and follow it back to the trailhead at the Badger Pass Ski Area.

Trailhead: From the junction with the Wawona Road at Chinquapin, drive up the Glacier Point Road 5 miles to the parking area at Badger Pass. Follow the blue signs to the upper parking lot, where you will find the Glacier Point Road trailhead.

Description: Begin your adventure by following the snow-covered Glacier Point Road north through light forest, observing the rules by avoiding the machine-set cross-country ski tracks that run all the way to Glacier Point. Follow the well-traveled road on a mild ascent for ¾ mile, to the beginning of a slight descent where you will find the signed Dewey Point Ridge Trail #14 to your left.

Leave the road and follow the marked trail into forest on a moderately steep initial climb. The grade eases a bit as you reach the top of a rise and then continue through the trees. Some level stretches of snowshoeing take you through sparse forest with limited views of the surrounding topography. The route undulates, periodically gaining the crest of low hills and rises, affording partial, tantalizing views of the Clark Range and the upper walls of Yosemite Valley. In the midst of a descent, you reach the well-signed junction with the Dewey Point Meadow Trail #18, at 2½ miles from the parking lot.

Remain on a northerly course as your route continues to climb and drop over and around more hills until a long descending traverse goes around a final hill and over to Dewey Point, 3 ½ miles from the trailhead. You stand at the very

View from Dewey Point

edge of the gaping cleft of Yosemite Valley, 3500 feet below. The view is incredible from this position directly across from the massive granite wall of El Capitan, with the Three Brothers just to its right. Immediately before you are the back sides of Leaning Tower, Cathedral Rocks and Cathedral Spires. On the northeast and east horizon, you can identify many of Yosemite's tallest mountains, such as Mt. Hoffman, Mt. Conness, and peaks of the Clark Range. This awe-inspiring view is the primary reason that a trip to Dewey Point is the quintessential Yosemite winter trip.

Unless preparations have been made to spend a night camped in the snow, you must tear yourself away from the magnificent scenery and begin the return trip toward Badger Pass. Retrace your previous steps for a mile back to the junction between Trails #14 and #18. For the loop option, follow #18 on a gentle journey through medium forest. A short but steeper descent across an open hillside leads to a long expanse of meadow. You proceed across the flat meadow, reaching the Glacier Point Road at the far end, 2½ miles from Dewey Point.

You can elect to simply follow the mundane new Glacier Point Road a little over a mile back to your vehicle, or you can head directly across Summit Meadow, making the short climb over the ridge and intersecting the Old Glacier Point Road 0.4 mile from its replacement. Once you reach the old road, turn southwest and follow the marked trail over inauspicious Badger Pass and down to the Badger Pass Ski Area, 1¼ miles from the Glacier Point Road and 7 miles from the starting point.

FYI: The cross-country ski center at Badger Pass rents snowshoes for $11.50 per day. If renting, note that snowshoes must be returned by 4:00 P.M. to avoid additional charges.

Warm-ups: Choices are limited, but the lodge at Badger Pass Ski Area does have a run-of-the-mill snack shop. On the second floor, an adult version serves assorted beers, limited hot drinks and nearly passable nachos and pizza. The snack shop is open from breakfast to 4:30 P.M. and the upstairs area is open from 11 to 5. For more refined cuisine, see the options in the Valley (Trips 9-15) or at the Wawona Hotel (Trip 1).

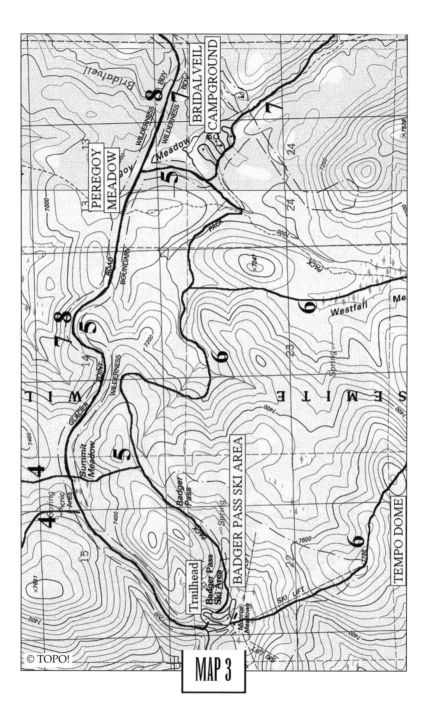

MAP 3

Trip 5

PEREGOY MEADOW LOOP

Duration: ¾ day
Distance: 6 ½ miles loop
Difficulty: Moderate
Elevation: 7180/6955/7475/7180
Maps: 3; *El Capitan & Half Dome* 7.5' quadrangles, 1990, 1992.
    Glacier Point Road Winter Trails

Introduction: For a relatively easy trip that doesn't tax your stamina or your routefinding abilities, try the Peregoy Meadow Loop. Using sections of marked trail in the Glacier Point Road system, this trip follows the gentle grade of the main road for the first 2 ¾ miles to scenic Peregoy Meadow. Leaving the Glacier Point Road at the meadows, the route follows the access road for ½ mile into isolated Bridalveil Campground, and then climbs up the old Glacier Point Road for most of the remaining 3 ¼ miles back to the parking lot at Badger Pass Ski Area. While not particularly steep, the last 3 miles back constitute a steady ascent, requiring the greatest physical effort of the trip.

Aside from the two clearings of Summit and Peregoy meadows, the trail passes through forested terrain for the entire journey. Absent the views of neighboring trips to Dewey and Glacier Points (Trips 4 & 8) or along the Merced Crest (Trip 5), you should have the trail to yourself once you leave the main Glacier Point Road. The quiet solitude along the forested sections of trail provides a stunning counterpoint to the crowded slopes at Badger Pass Ski Area.

Trailhead: Follow directions in Trip 4.

Description: From Badger Pass Ski Area, follow the mildly ascending Glacier Point Road through medium forest for ¾ mile. A subtle descent then leads quickly past the junction with the Dewey Point Ski Trail #14 (see Trip 4) and on to Summit Meadow, 1 mile from the parking lot.

Continue along the road on a very gentle climb for ¼ mile past Summit Meadow, until the road begins a 1 ½-mile long, mild, slightly winding descent. Just beyond the 2-mile mark, catch a glimpse of a portion of the Clark Range dead ahead up the road cut. As you continue down the Glacier Point Road, the descent ultimately leads to a junction at 2 ¾ miles for the signed winter trails emanating from Bridalveil Campground.

Turn south on the snow-covered access road into the campground, passing alongside a picturesque segment of Peregoy Meadow. A pleasant ½-mile stretch of road leads to the next winter trail junction, near the information board at the official entrance to the campground. Watch for a sign at the junction reading OLD GLACIER POINT ROAD, TO BADGER PASS 3.3.

Turn southwest onto the old Glacier Point Road and follow the gently graded path through light forest and down to a bridge across the tributary of Bridalveil Creek that drains Westfall Meadows. On a gradual climb away from the creek, you proceed along the road as it wraps around a hill through a light forest of pine. At the far end of the hill, where the road bends northwest, you reach a signed junction with the Limit Trail #13.

Travel along the old road to the end of the meadows and then follow a creek drainage around a hill to the south on a gentle grade. Soon you begin the long steady climb that eventually culminates at Badger Pass. While climbing moderately, you follow the path of the road as it winds around, reaching the next ski trail junction, where the grade eases at 5.3 miles. Signs indicate that you still have another 0.8 mile before reaching Badger Pass, while Summit Meadow lies just ½ mile north via the continuation of the Dewey Point Meadow Snow Trail #18.

A long gradual climb continues to Badger Pass. With no signs or views to indicate your arrival, the only way to realize you have actually reached the pass is by the slight downhill grade on the other side. Proceeding through light forest, following alongside a sloping meadow to the left, the grade of descent eventually increases. Glimpses of the Badger Pass Ski Area filter in and out of the trees until you finally break out of the forest into full view of the ski area. Shortly afterward, the old Glacier Point Road meets the upper loop of the parking area as the 6 ½-mile trip concludes.

FYI: Peregoy Meadow and Bridalveil Campground are excellent overnight destinations for snowshoers looking for a relatively leisurely trip to a campsite in the backcountry around Badger Pass. The mostly gentle terrain should be fairly easy for snowshoers with backpacks, a real bonus for an overnight snowcamp. Remember, all overnight stays in the Yosemite backcountry require a wilderness permit.

Warm-ups: See Trip 4.

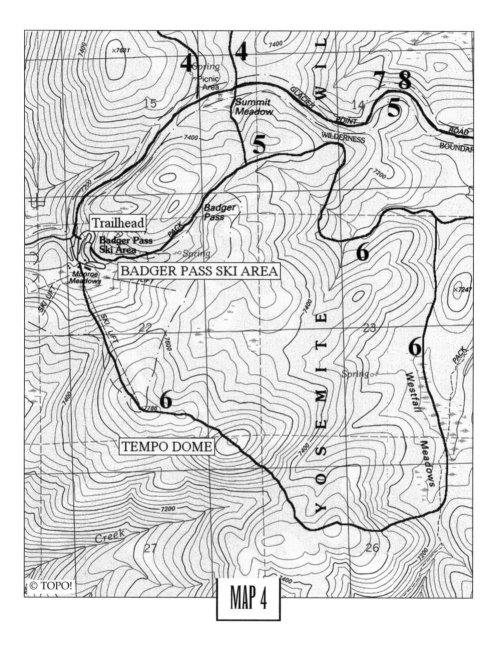

MAP 4

MERCED CREST LOOP

Duration: ¾ day
Distance: 6 miles loop trip
Difficulty: Moderate to difficult
Elevation: 7235/7845/7024/7470
Maps: 4; *El Capitan* 7.5' quadrangle, 1990
    Glacier Point Road Winter Trails

Introduction: Fine views, solitude and a peaceful meadow are just a few of the notable attributes to be found on this 6-mile loop. After gaining the ridge above Badger Pass Ski Area, snowshoers can gaze upon the high snowy peaks of the Clark Range, as well as Half Dome and the neighboring domes and peaks above Little Yosemite Valley. Thanks to the initial climb up the ski area and the undulating topography along the ridge beyond, most skiers intent on reaching distant Ostrander Lake choose simpler routes other than this one along the Merced Crest, thereby providing those souls willing to accept this challenge the opportunity to travel away from the crowds. Once you leave the Merced Crest Ski Trail and follow the Limit Trail, the nearly-mile-long expanse of Westfall Meadows provides snowshoers with a gentle journey through the quiet and scenic clearing. In addition to these highlights, much of the remaining trail passes through a quiet forest where snowshoers can experience the serenity of the winter landscape while listening only to the rhythmic crunch of their own snowshoes upon the pristine snow.

    Although the entire route follows marked winter trails in the Glacier Point Road system, minimizing the routefinding, the terrain is difficult enough to dissuade most beginners from attempting this journey. The steep climb up the slope of the ski area, gaining over 500 feet in ¾ mile, is the first obstacle to be overcome, followed by 2 miles of up-and-down snowshoeing along the ridge crest. Despite the gentle topography around Westfall Meadows past the crest section, most of the remainder of the trip beyond the meadows follows the old Glacier Point Road on a steady climb up to Badger Pass. Therefore, the scenery and solitude one can expect on this route should be enjoyed by snowshoers other than novices.

Those snowshoers who are willing to tackle the demands of the Merced Crest Loop will be treated to some of the prettiest scenery and most accessible seclusion to be found around the Badger Pass region. Just the contrast between the normal crowds of skiers at the starting point and the isolated backcountry beyond is an ample reward in itself.

Trailhead: Follow directions in Trip 4.

Description: From the Badger Pass Ski Area parking lot, follow the "Eagle" chairlift up the hillside through the ski area, avoiding the actual ski slopes and corresponding skiers as much as possible. Continue the steep ascent to the end of the lift at the top of the ridge, ¾ mile and 550 vertical feet from the parking lot, finding the beginning of the marked Merced Crest Ski Trail #16 heading southeast along the ridge top. Despite the absence of notable landmarks, the view from the top of the lift of the surrounding mountain ridges and canyons is quite scenic.

You proceed along the open crest for another ¼ mile until a short descent leads to a saddle. A steep climb up from the saddle leads directly to the summit of Tempo Dome, the high point of your journey at 7845 feet. Through the scattered trees that rim the dome there is a nice view of the Clark Range as well as a glimpse of Half Dome to the northeast.

With continued vistas, drop off the back side of Tempo Dome before a steeper angling descent leads into a light fir forest cover. Through the trees, paying close attention to the yellow rectangular

Gorgeous scenery ahead

markers to stay on route is needful. Eventually the trail bottoms out in a gully at the 1 ½-mile mark.

From the gully, a short moderate climb leads out of the forest to the top of an open hillside rimmed with trees. A brief descent followed by a slightly steeper and longer climb ascends the crest of the next hill. Strolling across the broad open hilltop, fine vistas are afforded of the Clark Range in addition to Liberty Cap, Mt. Broderick, Half Dome, the Quarter Domes and Clouds Rest across the gap of Little Yosemite Valley.

Heading directly toward the snow-capped peaks of the Clark Range, you continue along the Merced Crest Ski Trail as it gently drops over the crest of the hill. All too soon you bid farewell to the views as the route begins a more pronounced descent that diagonals across the hillside. Back into light forest, you continue down toward the basin directly south of Westfall Meadows, reaching a major ski trail junction just shy of the 2 ½-mile mark.

At the three-way junction, a set of yellow signs guides travelers toward their respective destinations. A grand adventure awaits those willing to make the longer journey east to Ostrander Lake along the continuation of the Merced Crest Ski Trail. However, your route

Enjoying the vista

bends north and follows the course of the Limit Trail #13 toward
Westfall Meadows. Almost immediately after turning north you
encounter a small pocket of meadow before reentering light forest.
This short forested section of trail is followed by the long graceful
expanse of the main body of Westfall Meadows.

In early summer Westfall Meadows becomes the wet, boggy
morass of semi-liquid earth capable of sucking the boots right off of
an unsuspecting hiker; but in winter a fresh blanket of snow allows
snowshoers and skiers to stroll or glide across the meadows with relative ease. The nearly level terrain and pleasant scenery combine to
create a very favorable setting for the ¾-mile journey across the
meadows. Toward the far end of Westfall Meadows follow the left-
hand branch of clearing into the trees.

From the edge of the meadows, you make a mild climb through
the forest to the gap directly west of point 7247 as shown on the *El
Capitan* topo map. After reaching the gap you begin a descent, heading north through the trees until a small, narrow meadow appears
about one-third mile from the gap. In the meadows, at 3 ¾ miles from
the trailhead, you encounter a signed junction with the marked trail
that follows the track of the old Glacier Point Road. Turning west at

the junction, follow directions in Trip 5 back along the Glacier Point Road to the Badger Pass Ski Area.

FYI: While some skiers forgo the initial climb up along the ski lift by purchasing a lift ticket from the lodge at Badger Pass, this practice certainly should be considered less than sporting.

Free transportation from Yosemite Valley to Badger Pass is available on a daily basis. Check with the front desk at Yosemite Lodge, Curry Village or the Ahwahnee Hotel, or the Visitor Center in Yosemite Village for more information.

Warm-ups: See Trip 4.

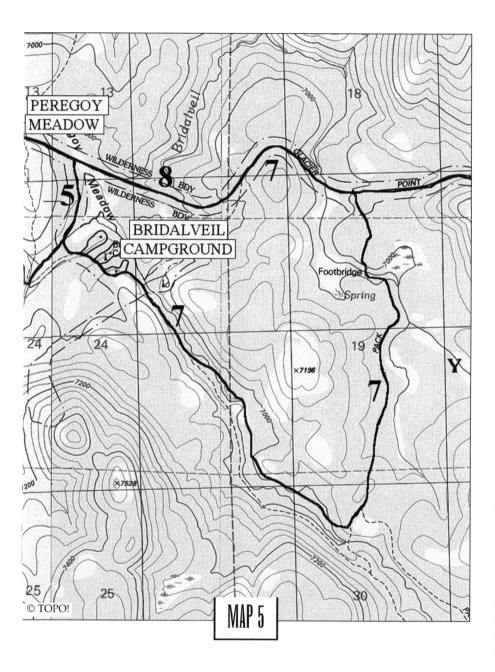

PEREGOY
MEADOW

BRIDALVEIL
CAMPGROUND

Footbridge

Spring

×7196

×7528

© TOPO!

MAP 5

GHOST FOREST LOOP

Duration: Full day
Distance: 1- mile loop trip
Difficulty: Difficult
Elevation: 7180/6940/7475
Maps: 5; *El Capitan & Half Dome* 7.5' quadrangles, 1990, 1992.
    Glacier Point Road Winter Trails

Introduction: As well as the pleasant scenery, the Ghost Forest Loop offers more experienced snowshoers the challenge of a longer trip. Even though the terrain is fairly gentle, the total distance of 11 miles is a good day's effort for even the hardiest of snowshoers. Thanks again to the network of marked winter trails radiating from Badger Pass Ski Area, the routefinding is minimal, although snowshoers should keep their eyes peeled for the yellow markers in a couple of critical locations.

The name of the loop derives from a 1987 fire that swept through the forest around Bridalveil Creek. Thankfully, the fire did not bring complete devastation to the surrounding forest, and travelers can get an eyewitness view of scorched trees intermixed with those still alive.

Trailhead: Follow directions in Trip 4.

Description: Follow directions in Trip 5 to the junction with the access road into Bridalveil Campground at Peregoy Meadow, 2 ¾ miles from Badger Pass.

73

Rather than heading toward Bridalveil Campground as in Trip 5, remain on the Glacier Point Road, making a short climb away from Peregoy Meadow. Soon you follow the road on a gentle descent to a crossing of Bridalveil Creek. Beyond the creek, climb moderately up the tree-lined road, passing through a section of burned timber from a 1987 fire. You continue the ascent, reaching a signed junction with the Ghost Forest Loop/Bridalveil Creek Snow Trail #21 at 4 miles from the trailhead.

Leaving the wide swath of the Glacier Point Road, follow the marked trail on a gentle grade through a mixture of living and burned lodgepole pine trees. A mixture of orange and yellow rectangular markers guides you along the nearly level trail to a crossing of the creek on a wooden footbridge. Then go alongside the creek for a half-mile or so, until the trail veers away and comes to a signed junction just past the 5½-mile mark.

At the **Y**-junction, take the right-hand branch following the signed directions to 19 CAMPGROUND 2.0. A short decline leads quickly to a westward bend in the trail—watch for yellow markers. A fair distance away from but paralleling the main channel of Bridalveil Creek, you follow the route through a sparse ponderosa-pine forest on a gentle decline. Eventually you reach a narrow clearing that slopes toward the creek. Cross the clearing and pick up the marked route on the far side near a sign reading: 19 GHOST FOREST LOOP, GLACIER POINT ROAD 1.

Beyond the clearing, follow the trail alongside the creek, eventually crossing to the west side, which should not present any potential difficulties until early spring. You continue next to the creek for most of the remainder of your journey to Bridalveil Campground. Once at the Campground, follow the access road to the signed junction (OLD GLACIER POINT ROAD, TO BADGER PASS 3.3) with the old Glacier Point Road. On the way through the camp, pass the junction with Trail #23, which leads southwest 1 mile to a connection with the Limit Trail in Westfall Meadows.

From the old Glacier Point Road junction, turn west onto the road and follow directions in Trip 5 back to Badger Pass.

FYI: If time is of the essence and there isn't a broken trail up the old Glacier Point Road, you can continue along the access road from Bridalveil Campground ½ mile out to the newer Glacier Point Road and follow your own tracks back to Badger Pass Ski Area.

Warm-ups: See Trip 4.

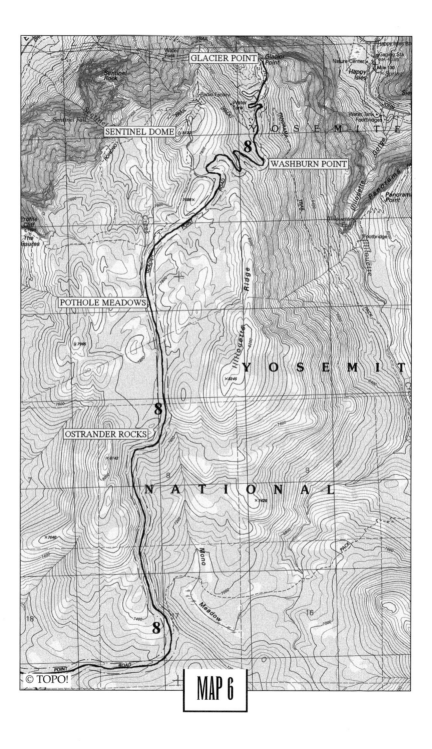

GLACIER POINT

SENTINEL DOME

WASHBURN POINT

POTHOLE MEADOWS

YOSEMIT

OSTRANDER ROCKS

NATIONAL

© TOPO!

MAP 6

GLACIER POINT

Duration: 2-4 days
Distance: 21-mile round trip
Difficulty: Difficult
Elevation: 7180/7830/7214
Maps: 3, 5 & 6; *El Capitan & Half Dome* 7.5' quadrangles, 1990, 1992
Glacier Point Road Winter Trails

Introduction: Thousands of tourists make the trek up the Glacier Point Road for the superb views virtually every summer day between Memorial Day and Labor Day. Buses and cars fill the parking lot, and the short trail to the viewpoint is lined with examples from the full gamut of humanity. After the road is closed by the approaching snows of winter, the once-busy tourist stop is left in solitude for the hearty few willing to travel the 10 ½ miles under their own power. The absolutely incredible views are just as magnificent, nearly 3200 feet above Yosemite Valley, but the added tranquility of a winter visit makes the experience almost too good to be true.

There certainly is a cost to be paid for the extraordinary opportunity to stand on the edge of Glacier Point in the winter, peering into the deep chasm of Yosemite Valley and gazing across the horizon above the lofty peaks that form the Sierra Crest. That price is the long trip required just to reach the view. Skiers have the advantage of a machine-set track thanks to the Park Service, but snowshoers will have to make their own way along the 10 ½-mile route. All but the superhuman will need a minimum of two days for the trip out and back, and extra days would possibly make the journey more enjoy-

77

able. A multi-day outing would provide extra time for visiting other points of interest along the way, including stops at Taft Point and Sentinel Dome.

Any overnight excursion into the Yosemite backcountry during winter will require additional planning and equipment, and an accurate weather forecast. An extended period of fair weather during the longer days of late winter or early spring can provide the basis for a particularly exceptional adventure. A successful snowshoe trip to the outstanding view from Glacier Point can be the ultimate Yosemite experience.

Trailhead: Follow directions in Trip 4.

Description: Follow directions in Trips 5 and 7 to the junction of the Glacier Point Road and the Ghost Forest Loop/Bridalveil Creek Snow Trail #21.

Heading east, stay on the Glacier Point Road, climbing moderately through a light pine forest interspersed with more dead timber from the 1987 fire. A ¾-mile climb from the junction leads to the Horizon Ridge Ski Trail #15, one of the three marked routes to Ostrander Lake. Continue ascending the path of the winding road as it bends north, passing a sign for MONO MEADOWS at 5 miles from the Badger Pass Ski Area parking lot. One-half mile farther up the road, past the half-way point of the journey to Glacier Point, fine views begin to filter through the scattered pines of Mt. Starr King, Mt. Clark and other peaks and domes of the Clark Range.

The moderate climb continues until the 7-mile mark, where easier terrain makes for pleasant snowshoeing over the next couple of miles. Proceeding up the road, you pass Pothole Meadows and begin to see the striking hulk of Sentinel Dome. At 8 miles from the parking lot, you reach the summer trailhead for the 1-mile hike to Sentinel Dome and the 1 ¼-mile hike to Taft Point. If this is a multi-day adventure and time is available for these side trips, the views are more than rewarding. Although the navigation is straightforward, the route to Taft Point has the advantage of being marked for winter travel.

Beyond the Sentinel Dome and Taft Point trailhead, the Glacier Point Road begins a twisting descent that lasts most of the way to

Glacier Point. Passing through a forest primarily of red fir, the narrow, serpentine road closely follows the route of the original Glacier Point wagon road built in 1882. The winding descent through the trees is briefly interrupted at 9 ½ miles by a spectacular vista over the precipitous cliffs at Washburn Point. Not only can the sweeping ridge of peaks along the Clark Range be seen directly to the east, but Half Dome is clearly visible to the northeast as well.

Away from Washburn Point, the road continues to snake down toward the Glacier Point parking lot. You have another spectacular view around a big sweeping curve before arriving at the parking area, 10 ¼ miles from the starting point at Badger Pass. Glacier Point itself is another ¼ mile north. To call the view from the point spectacular seems entirely inadequate.

FYI: A guided tour to Glacier Point can be arranged with overnight dormitory-style accommodations at the recently constructed Glacier Point Winter Lodge. Call the Yosemite Cross-Country Ski Center & Ski School at (209) 372-8444 for more information. Snow camping in the Yosemite backcountry requires a wilderness permit, obtainable at the Badger Pass Ski Area or the Valley visitor center.

Warm-ups: See Trip 4.

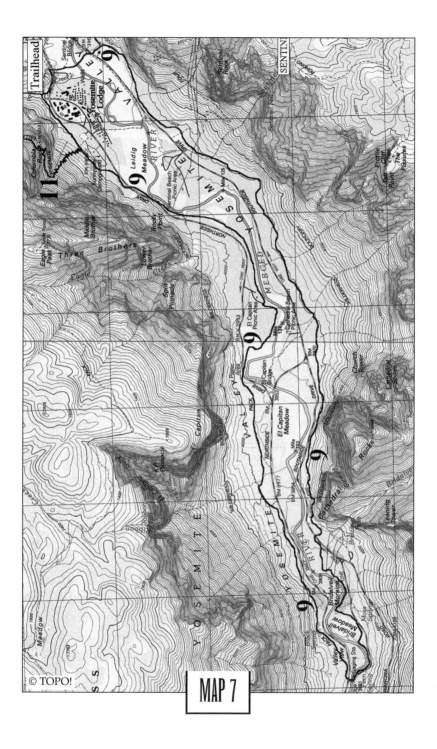

MAP 7

YOSEMITE VALLEY
WEST LOOP

Duration: Full day
Distance: 11-mile loop trip
Difficulty: Easy to moderate
Elevation: 3970/3870/4065
Map: 7; *Half Dome & Yosemite Falls* 7.5' quadrangles, 1992
  Topographic Map of Yosemite Valley 1:24,000 scale, published by
  Wilderness Press, 1993

Introduction: On those infrequent occasions when an adequate layer of snow blankets Yosemite Valley, a more attractive setting in which to snowshoe is hard to imagine. Fresh snow on the Valley floor, on the ledges of the vertical granite walls, and atop the Valley rim transforms the gorge into a veritable winter wonderland. The hush created by new-fallen snow combines with the greatly reduced number of winter visitors to produce a serene setting totally outside the experience of those who visit the Park in other seasons. Common Yosemite landmarks are still here, their stunning beauty accented by a blanket of powder, but gone are the crowds and the congestion.

Due to variations in snowfall, planning a snowshoe trip for Yosemite Valley is a highly speculative proposition. Average winters will definitely see significant accumulations of snow at times, but trying to determine those periods ahead of time is tricky work. Once a cold Pacific storm leaves a sufficient layer of snow in the 3900-foot.

valley, typically moderate temperatures are not too far behind. Consequently, the snow that does fall in the Valley doesn't hang around for extended periods. Snow in Yosemite Valley usually is in good condition for a few days at most, quickly turning into a wet mush and then melting altogether not long afterward. Snowshoers wishing to tramp in the Valley will need to pay special attention to the weather when planning their trip.

When adequate snowfall is present, snowshoers can take advantage of the highly developed network of hiking trails that criss-cross the Valley floor, making any number of short, medium or long trips possible. While the West Valley Loop described here is 11 miles long, options are available for shortening the trip. The west end of the loop provides the best opportunity for solitude, while the east end offers considerably less, especially around the bustling Yosemite Village and Yosemite Lodge areas.

El Capitan from trail

Trailhead: Until plans are implemented prohibiting visitors without overnight reservations from driving private vehicles into Yosemite Valley, parking is available at the Day-Use Parking area near Curry Village. Whichever of the three main highways snow-shoers follow to the Valley, ultimately they will end up on Southside Drive, the two-lane, one-way road that leads all motorists into the valley. Follow signs to the Day Use Parking Area near Curry Village and park in the lot as space is available.

From stop #14 (Curry Village) next to the parking area, free shuttle buses run every 20 minutes and go to 14 other stops throughout the Valley. From stop #14, or other points in the Valley, ride the shuttle bus to stop #7 (Yosemite Falls) and follow the description below. During the winter, buses do not run to stops #15-18 (Upper Pines Campground, Happy Isles, Mirror Lake & Stables).

Because of frequent bear problems, do not leave any food, anything that looks like food, or anything that has an odor in the car overnight. Bear-proof lockers are provided in the parking area for any suspect items.

Description: From the Yosemite Falls Parking Lot (Bus Stop #7), find the Valley Loop Trail behind the restroom building, signed: EL CAPITAN 3.2, TOP OF YOSEMITE FALLS 3.8. You head southwest on a nearly level grade through light forest, paralleling the Northside Road. Pass Swan Slab, which provides a nice practice area for novice climbers, and reach a junction with the Yosemite Falls Trail (see Trip 8) at ½ mile.

From the junction, you continue through light forest and boulders, passing above Sunnyside Campground. Climbers from bygone days remember this site as Camp 4, the camping haven for rock climbers who flocked to the valley in the 60's, lured by the prospects of the increasing popular big-wall climbing. Even today, climbers make up the majority of people camped at Sunnyside.

Beyond Sunnyside, you draw closer to the road and eventually cross to the south side of the highway, skirting Leidig Meadow. Nearing the Merced River there are fine views of North Dome, Royal Arches, Clouds Rest and the upper part of Half Dome. Soon you reenter light forest of ponderosa pine, incense cedar and black oak, leaving the views behind. Cross Eagle Creek on a wooden bridge and come to a small clearing with a splendid view of El Capitan. Continue along the easy grade of the trail, reaching a junction with an unsigned lateral trail.

Soon entering another small meadow, you have nice views of El Capitan, Three Brothers and Cathedral Rocks. Continue along the trail as it follows the course of the Merced River, passing the El Capitan Picnic Area and bending around to meet the Northside Road once again. Follow the road for a short distance and then cross to the north side. A sign at the crossing reads: EL CAPITAN 0.4, BRIDALVEIL 4.1.

Paralleling the road, you v alk through a tunnel of young cedars, quickly crossing a wide road providing access for climbers to El Capitan. Walking beneath the massive wall of El Capitan, thoughts of the effort involved in climbing such a face flood your mind. Cross another climber's access road and then quickly come to a **Y**-junction, 3 miles from your staring point. The left-handtrail heads south to the El Capitan Bridge. If a shorter loop is desired, see FYI below.

For the full loop, take the right-hand branch at the junction, following a sign marked BRIDALVEIL FALL 3.7, POHONO BRIDGE 1.9. Proceed along the trail as it veers away from the highway on a slight climb. Aside from the periodic traffic noise, this stretch of trail is quiet and peaceful. At 4 miles, cross Ribbon Falls Creek. Beyond the creek you reach a road which leads to a wood-cutting area. Follow the trail as it angles back toward and then runs parallel to the highway. As the west end of the valley narrows, the trail, the road, and the river come closer to one another, as they must share a shrinking piece of valley floor. The increased sound of the tumbling water in the Merced River indicates that the nearly level grade of the upper valley has increased here as well. You continue through light forest, eventually sighting the Pohono Bridge ahead. After a short descent, you curve down to the road and cross the Pohono Bridge, 5 ¼ miles from the Yosemite Falls parking area.

After you cross the Pohono Bridge, find the resumption of the Valley Loop Trail just above the south bank of the river. Go upstream ¼ mile until the trail veers south away from the river to circumvent Bridalveil Meadow. Near the meadow, there are pleasant views of El Capitan, Cathedral Rocks, Leaning Tower and Dewey, Crocker, Stanford and Old Inspiration points. The trail parallels the Southside Road about 20 feet from the pavement to the far end of the meadow, where it heads back toward the river through light forest. You follow the peaceful river on its winding course with nice views of Half Dome and El Capitan across the waters. Following the river, the trail circles back around to the roadway but quickly veers away again.

The next potential obstacle is the crossing of multi-channeled Bridalveil Creek. If the temperatures have been cold and the flow of water is low, ford the channels and proceed up the route of the trail. However, if warmer conditions have increased the amount of water, a better option is to avoid the fords by going alongside the road to the resumption of the trail beyond the last channel of Bridalveil Creek. Whichever way is chosen, past the creek the trail comes back besides the road for 200 yards, eventually crossing the Southside Road near the V14 road marker at the Bridalveil Falls viewpoint, 6 ½ miles from the Yosemite Falls parking area.

Just past the road is a T-junction, the right-hand trail leading back to Bridalveil Falls. Bear left and quickly come to a Y-junction. Veer right following signed directions for CURRY VILLAGE 5.5, STABLES 6.0. From the junction, make a moderate climb above the river and the road across a rocky slope directly below Cathedral Rocks. Traveling through light forest, the climb soon abates; follow the trail on a moderate descent back toward the road. The floor of the Valley starts to widen again as you proceed up the canyon on a slight rise. Reach another T-junction at the 8-mile mark. Traditional Yosemite signs of metal with cut-out letters give the following destinations and mileages: EL CAPITAN 1.4, YOSEMITE FALLS 4.0, STABLES 6.7 (left, southwest) and CAMP CURRY 3.9, STABLES 4.4 (straight ahead, east-northeast).

From the junction, proceed straight ahead into a lighter forest cover where there are nice views of El Capitan and the Three Brothers on the north wall and Cathedral Spires on the south. Back into trees, the views diminish as a mild climb is made up the Valley. Continue up the mildly graded trail, getting your first glimpse through the trees of Yosemite Falls. After crossing Sentinel Creek, approach a small clearing for a grand view across the Valley of Yosemite Falls. A short distance farther, you encounter a junction with the Fourmile Trail at 9 ½ miles. Closed in winter, the Fourmile Trail climbs steeply from the Valley floor up to Glacier Point.

From the junction continue heading northeast on the mildly graded trail, still enjoying some fine views across the Valley. The road draws near once more as you approach the Swinging Bridge Picnic Area on the opposite side of the highway. Soon you head back into light forest and then pass behind the Yosemite Chapel, the oldest structure in the Valley. At the far end of the chapel grounds, you reach a 3-way trail junction at 10 ½ miles.

Turn left (northwest) at the junction and head out toward the road. You cross Southside Road and follow the trail through the meadows and over a footbridge. Continue across the meadows to the path across Northside Road, turn left (west) and proceed down to the Yosemite Falls Parking lot.

FYI: For a shorter variation, 3 ½ miles of the loop can be shaved off by turning south from the **Y**-junction 3 miles from Yosemite Falls and following that trail out to the Northside Road. Walk down the road and across the El Capitan Bridge, from where there is an excellent view of Cathedral Rocks, finding the continuation of the trail just beyond the bridge. Then head east and then southeast to a crossing of the Southside Road. Once across the road, proceed up the trail to a junction with the Valley Loop Trail, ¾ mile from the **Y**-junction.

Warm-ups: For those dinner patrons tired of the a la carte prices and the mundane food at the cafeteria, the Mountain Room at Yosemite Lodge offers tired snowshoers a pleasant change. Enjoy the splendid views of Yosemite Falls while seated cozily in the newly remodeled

View of El Capitan from Dewey Point

restaurant, and sit back and relax while waiters deliver superbly broiled steaks, creative seafood dishes, or pasta specialties to your table. Warm sourdough bread accompanies each meal, and the dinner salads are made with a mixture of fresh greens (I recommend the raspberry vinaigrette dressing). The wine list is more than passable, and even the desserts provide plenty of tantalizing temptations.

The Mountain Room is open daily from 5 to 9 P.M. The prices range from moderate to moderately expensive, and major credit cards are accepted. Reservations and long waits are both unheard of during the winter months. The accepted dress is casual.

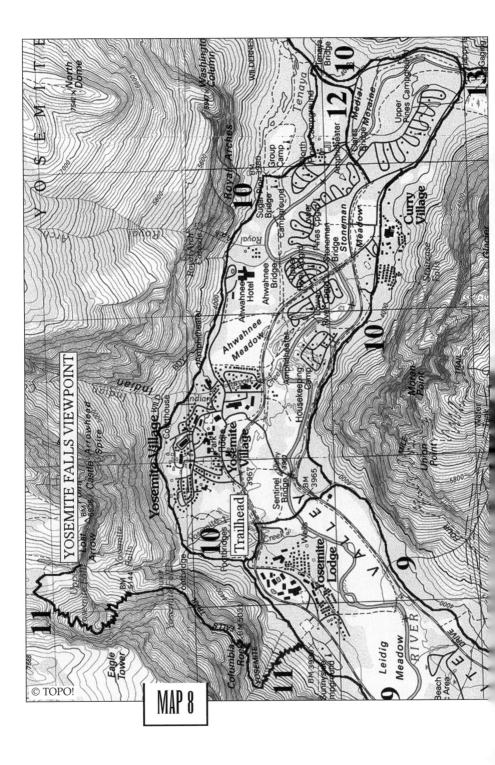

YOSEMITE FALLS VIEWPOINT

MAP 8

© TOPO!

YOSEMITE VALLEY
EAST LOOP

Duration: ¾ day
Distance: 6 ¼ miles loop trip
Difficulty: Easy to moderate
Elevation: 3970/4170
Maps: 8; *Half Dome & Yosemite Falls* 7.5' quadrangles, 1992
Topographic Map of Yosemite Valley 1:24,000 scale, published by Wilderness Press, 1993

Introduction: Compared to the West Loop, this route offers less in the way of solitude, as along the way you pass by a number of bustling centers of activity, including Curry Village, the Ahwahnee Hotel, and Yosemite Village. However, many sections of trail away from these areas are lightly used, particularly when a blanket of snow carpets the ground. Forested areas beside the Merced River or Tenaya Creek can be quite peaceful. This trip offers some fine views of some of Yosemite's famous landmarks, such as Yosemite Falls, Royal Arches and Half Dome.

Following the Valley floor for the great part of the journey, this loop trip requires little elevation gain and the routefinding is straightforward. Classic Yosemite cut-out metal signs provide travelers with plenty of directions at all major junctions. As on the West Loop, connecting trails and roads offer many shortcuts and variations. If you happen to be in the Valley when the snow conditions are ideal, this trip provides a fairly easy and enjoyable experience.

Trailhead: Follow directions in Trip 9 to the Yosemite Falls bus stop #7.

Description: From the parking lot at Yosemite Falls, you proceed east toward Yosemite Village on the bike/pedestrian path that parallels Northside Road. After 0.2 mile, turn south, crossing the road and heading out into the meadow. You follow the path across a footbridge over the Merced River and continue to the crossing of Southside Road near Yosemite Chapel, ½ mile from your starting point. Behind the chapel, locate the **T** trail junction and turn northeast up the left-hand branch.

You walk through an area of boulders and oaks, following the trail as it winds around, eventually drawing near to the road in more of an evergreen forest. Your trail joins the bike path as you follow directly alongside the right edge of the pavement for nearly ¼ mile, before the hiking path veers away from the road to the right. At this point a sign reads: CURRY VILLAGE .9, STABLES 1.4.

Climbing briefly above the road, you pass the ramshackle Housekeeping Camp across the road; this eyesore is slated for closure soon. Near the end of the camp, but on your side of the road, is the LeConte Memorial. Operated by the Sierra Club, the memorial was built in honor of Joseph LeConte, an eminent Berkeley geologist who linked the formation of Yosemite Valley to glaciation. The memorial originally occupied a site in Curry Village and served as the Valley's first visitor center, but was relocated to the current site in 1919.

The bike path and the hiking trail coincide again briefly near the memorial. Then you veer off away from the road, following the trail into the forest again. Soon you reach the outskirts of Curry Village and head along the paved sidewalk in front of the main entrance. You continue along the walkway past the hamburger stand, the mountaineering school, and the tent cabins at the far end of the village. Paralleling the fire lane, you follow the trail back into forest, passing the wilderness-permit-holders parking area to your right and Upper Pines Campground to your left. Just past the 2 ½-mile mark, you come to Happy Isles Nature Center. The center is closed during winter, but the bathrooms remain open all year.

Leaving Happy Isles, you walk along the road across the Happy Isles Bridge spanning the Merced River and find the continuation of the unmarked Valley Loop Trail just a short distance east from the paved road where it loops around to the north. You follow the trail as it parallels the road, the Merced River within earshot. Pass underneath a large overhanging rock and veer away from the road for nearly ½ mile until you come to a trail junction near the Tenaya Bridge, 3.3 miles from your starting point.

At the junction, you turn left and cross the closed road to Mirror Lake, following a sign: STABLES 0.5, YOSEMITE FALLS 2.8. Soon you walk along Tenaya Creek, from where you have fine views of Washington Column and the Royal Arches on the north valley wall. Quickly, at 3 ¾ miles, you come to the stables, and as you enter the compound, you must bear sharply to the right (northwest), following a sign reading: INDIAN CAVES .9, YOSEMITE FALLS 2.0, EL CAPITAN 5.3.

In light to moderate forest cover, you pass North Pines Campground, cross Tenaya Creek on a foot bridge and reach another junction, near the 4-mile mark. Continue straight through the campground and immediately find yet another trail junction just across the paved road. Turn left (west) at the junction, following directions on a sign for YOSEMITE FALLS 2.0, EL CAPITAN 5.3.

As you walk through light forest, more views of Royal Arches await you on the steep wall above. Drop down to the Ahwahnee Hotel, ½ mile from the junction, veering to the right just before reaching the edge of the parking lot. As the trail parallels the road into the hotel grounds, you pass through another field of large granite boulders. Proceeding along the route, not far from the road, you have pleasant views across Ahwahnee Meadows to the south wall of the Valley. After a brief glimpse of the upper part of Yosemite Falls, your route drops into the Church Bowl area, 5 miles from the beginning.

Leaving Church Bowl, the trail turns away from the road and begins to climb. You cross Indian Canyon Creek on a small wooden bridge and continue the moderate climb as the trail winds across the hillside. After one-third mile of climbing, the trail begins a lengthy descent, but not before you have a nice view of the Valley. As you descend, the route passes behind the numerous buildings of Yosemite Village. Ignore a lateral trail heading down to some stables on your left and continue the descent to the end of the village, where you find another T-junction at 5 ¾ miles.

You continue straight ahead at the junction, toward the bridge at the base of Lower Yosemite Falls. An easy stroll leads to the bridge, and then you follow the path as it curves around alongside a branch of Yosemite Creek. Walk along the path to your beginning point at the Yosemite Falls parking lot.

FYI: Adequate snow cover in the valley occurs sporadically throughout the winter—refer to comments in the Introduction of Trip 9.

Warm-ups: The dress code along with the potential amount of your check are quite enough to dissuade the average snowshoer from venturing into the dining room at the Ahwahnee Hotel for dinner. However, casual dress is acceptable for breakfast and lunch, and the prices, while certainly not a bargain, are not nearly as stiff for these meals. Besides, the food is superb and the atmosphere is unmatched. You might be fortunate enough to be seated at a table with a floor-to-ceiling view of Yosemite Falls. For a fantastic carbo-loading, pre-snowshoe warm-up, try the blueberry pancakes. I'm pretty sure the coffee isn't the same stuff you find at the other restaurants in the valley, but if it is, then the classic Ahwahnee cups must be responsible for improving the taste.

The Ahwahnee dining room is open for breakfast from 7 A.M. to 10:30 A.M. and for lunch from 11:30 A.M. to 2:30 P.M. If you're tempted to try the Sunday brunch, my advice is to skip it unless you can eat such great quantities of food as to get your money's worth.

Trip 11

YOSEMITE FALLS

Duration: ¾ day
Distance: 7 ½-mile round trip
Difficulty: Moderate to difficult
Elevation: 3970/6935
Maps: 8; *Half Dome & Yosemite Falls* 7.5' quadrangles, 1992
Topographic Map of Yosemite Valley 1;24,000 scale, published by
Wilderness Press, 1993

Introduction: The trail to the top of Yosemite Falls is one of the few
trails climbing out of the Valley that the Park Service keeps open during the winter. When conditions are warm, you may be able to hike
all the way up the south-facing wall of the canyon to the falls without snowshoes. At other times, you may have to carry your snowshoes for a considerable distance, till there's enough snow.
Occasionally, you will be able to snowshoe all the way from the valley floor. Whatever surface you travel over on your way to the lip of
the falls at the end of your 3 ¾-mile journey, the scenery is both
breathtaking and awe-inspiring.

   If a heavy snowpack coincides with unusually warm temperatures, you may see Yosemite Falls in all their glory, but more likely
the falls will be frozen or barely running in an average winter. The
beauty is just as dramatic, though, as the falls freeze into an icy column of water, ledges and clefts of the Valley wall are dusted with
powder, and a slanting apron of snow rests at the base of the upper
fall; all these elements combine to create a splendidly photogenic dis-

play. Standing at the lip of the upper falls, you peer straight down the face of this winter scene, 3000 feet to the valley below.

Trailhead: Follow directions in Trip 9 to the Yosemite Falls bus stop #7.

Description: Follow directions in Trip 9 to the junction between the Valley Loop and Yosemite Falls trails, ½ mile from the Yosemite Falls parking lot.

From the junction, you head up the slope to a series of over 40 short switchbacks that zigzag up the talus slope beneath a moderate cover of oaks. After about 500 feet of elevation gain, you reach a streambed, where you have your first view across Leidig Meadow to the far Valley wall.

More switchbacks lead to the viewpoint at Columbia Rock, 1 ½ miles from the starting point. Half Dome, Quarter Domes and Cathedral Rocks are just a few of the major landmarks visible from this viewpoint. You continue up the trail via a few more switchbacks until the trail straightens out, traversing northeast across the hillside. After a mild drop, the trail bends north to a sudden and dramatic view of Upper Yosemite Fall.

The climb resumes as you follow the trail up a steep trough adjacent to the fall. Around the 2-mile mark, you encounter even more switchbacks as you continue the ascent of the trough. Another mile of climbing brings you into a gully and a junction with the Eagle Peak Trail.

At the junction, turn right and make a short climb out of the gully and up onto a broad hilltop. From here, turn south and follow the crest almost all the way out to the rim of the Valley. Just before the rim, bear east and descend steps toward Yosemite Creek and then down to the viewpoint. Once you have had your fill of the dramatic view of the precipitous plunge down the sheer face of the fall, return to the parking lot.

FYI: For a more adventurous trip, you could follow the course of the summer trail over to Yosemite Point for a spectacular vista. From the fall, return to the crest and descend to Yosemite Creek. From the creek climb out of the drainage and then circle around to the point.

Warm-ups: After a chilly day in the backcountry, the Mountain Room Lounge in Yosemite Lodge provides snowshoers with the possibility of a warm spot next to a roaring fire, a fine setting for enjoying a hot drink or a snifter of brandy. During winter, the lounge is open 5-9:30 P.M. during weekdays and noon-10 P.M. on Saturday and Sunday.

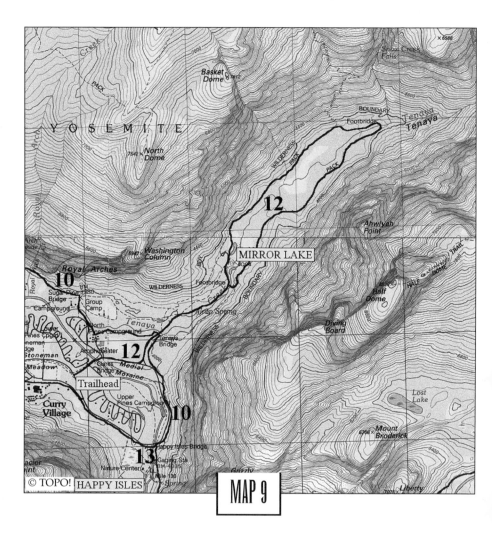

MAP 9

MIRROR LAKE
TENAYA CANYON LOOP

Duration: ½ day
Distance: 6 ½ miles loop trip
Difficulty: Easy
Elevation: 4000/4120
Maps: 9; *Half Dome* 7.5' quadrangle, 1992
       Topographic Map of Yosemite Valley 1:24,000 scale, published by
       Wilderness Press, 1993

Introduction: Depending on the current conditions, you may find enough snow in the Valley to successfully call this journey a snowshoe trip. Even if you have to walk the road to Mirror Lake, during most winters you should have many days of adequate snowpack in the canyon above the lake. The nearly level grade, combined with the fact that you can't get lost unless you make a steep climb out of the canyon, makes this trip well-suited for snowshoers ready to break away from marked winter trails.

Like most popular Valley destinations, Mirror Lake is a tourist magnet during the warmer months of the year. Throngs of visitors walk the road or bicycle part way, drawn at least in part by images of days gone by when Mirror Lake lived up to its name. Almost anyone who has seen any pictures of Yosemite at all has gazed upon the reflection of Half Dome in the tranquil waters of Mirror Lake. Unfortunately, these glory days are past, as the lake has been reduced

97

to a fraction of its former size. However, the area is still beautiful, the classic face of Half Dome still rises triumphantly over the canyon, and winter images still attract scores of photographers, making Mirror Lake a must-see event for all winter visitors.

Away from Mirror Lake, in the upper reaches of Tenaya Canyon the number of people diminishes drastically. Unfortunately, the bridge across Tenaya Creek at the far end of the canyon was destroyed during the New Year's flood of '97. Until repairs are completed, snowshoers will have to retrace their steps, rather than being able to finish the loop. Check with Park officials regarding the status of repairs before you begin your journey.

Trailhead: Follow directions in Trip 9 to the Day Use Parking Area at Curry Village, or travel on the shuttle bus to stop #19 (Lower Pines Campground.

Description: If you parked your vehicle at the Day Use Parking Area, walk northeast down the road a short distance to shuttle bus stop #19. From bus stop #19, travel over Clarks Bridge spanning the Merced River and follow signs for HAPPY ISLES .8, MIRROR LAKE 1.2, which point the way up a closed paved road. Soon you come to a **Y** and take the left-hand branch signed MIRROR LAKE 1. After a while, reach another **Y**-junction near a restroom and bear right, following a sign reading MIRROR LAKE .6. As you continue along the road, the looming face of Half Dome comes into view, after which the road draws near to Tenaya Creek. The grade of the road increases as you climb toward Mirror Lake. Where the road ends, 1 ¼ mile from the bus stop, there are another restroom and a pay phone. Just beyond, the wide path of the Mirror Lake Trail begins.

Nearby is Mirror Lake, or at least what is left of Mirror Lake. There remains a large enough portion of a still pond to catch a reflection of Half Dome in the water's surface if you can gain the right angle, but there is no doubt that the fame of Mirror Lake lies in its former glory. In the recent past, scientists thought that the lake was filling in with sediment, becoming a meadow in a natural progression. Nowadays, they theorize that the "lake" is a pool in a seasonal stream, affected by the speed and volume of the stream flow, which deposits and scours sand from the pool in cycles. So, who knows? Maybe one day Mirror Lake will regain grand stature.

Just after the beginning of the trail, a short lateral trail leads over to the shore of Mirror Lake and quickly loops back around to the main trail, providing convenient access for those desiring a closer view. Past the lake, where the main trail passes through a rock slide below steep granite cliffs, you have a nice view across the canyon of Half Dome. Quickly, you head back into light forest and come alongside the creek for a short spell before veering away once again. Proceed through light forest until, a mile from Mirror Lake, you reach a junction with the Tenaya Lake & Tuolumne Meadows Trail. Near the junction one of the classic old iron signs with cut-out letters lists destinations and mileages.

Beyond the junction, storm damage has closed the trail until repairs can be made to the bridge across Tenaya Creek one-third mile farther up the trail. The bridge was destroyed during the infamous New Year's flood of '97, evidence of which is the boulders and debris deposited in the stream channel on your right. Until reconstruction is completed, you can parallel Tenaya Creek up to the bridge site, but you won't be able to cross the creek.

Once the bridge has been replaced, you can follow the route on the opposite bank back down past the meadows, Mirror Lake, the artificial dam and a pond to the footbridge which heads back over Tenaya Creek, closing the loop at the junction with the paved road. From there, retrace your steps down the closed road to the bus stop.

FYI: Mirror Lake was called Ahwiyah by the original residents of the Valley. The name means "quiet water," which is perhaps a better appellation for the current condition of the lake.

Warm-ups: The pizza at Degnan's Fast Food in Yosemite Village may not be on a par with the styles found at gourmet eateries in New York, Chicago, or San Francisco, but if you're dying for a pizza-fix, you can get one from 11 A.M. to 4 P.M. While the quality of the pizza may be average at best, you can wash it down with some fine beers from the deli next door. You can also find a host of other fast-food items at Degnan's.

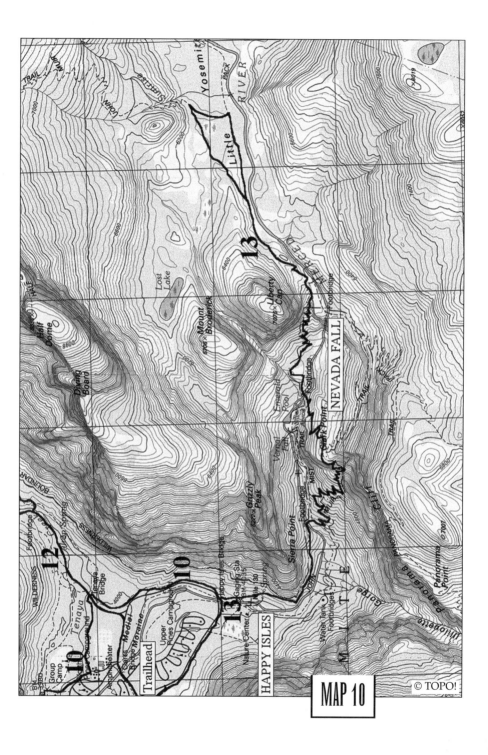

MAP 10

© TOPO!

LITTLE YOSEMITE VALLEY

Duration: Full day
Distance: 10 ¼ miles round trip to Little Yosemite Valley
       11 ½ miles round trip to Little Yosemite Valley Campgrounds
Difficulty: Difficult
Elevation: 3980/6150
Maps: 10; *Half Dome* 7.5' quadrangle, 1992
       Topographic Map of Yosemite Valley 1:24,000 scale, published by
       Wilderness Press, 1993

Introduction: Too cold for tourists, too steep for skiers, the winter route past Vernal and Nevada falls into Little Yosemite Valley is the gateway into the Yosemite backcountry for experienced snowshoers. While hordes of visitors march up the Mist Trail like a parade of ants nearly every summer day, very few souls entertain the idea of venturing into the snow-covered reaches of the canyon during winter. The overwhelming majority of the few winter visitors who do venture up the trail are typically content to go no farther than the Vernal Fall Bridge. Most cross-country skiers frown at the prospect of having to either ski the treacherous route or pack their skis that far up the trail to reach decent skiing conditions. For those willing to endure the climb up the steep canyon, Little Yosemite Valley offers snowshoers a rare opportunity to enjoy the beautiful scenery devoid of crowds.

    The Park Service wisely closes the section of the Mist Trail from the Vernal Fall Bridge to the trail junction below Nevada Fall during winter and early spring, as well as the section of the John Muir Trail above Clark Point. Not that many years ago, a massive slide occurred

Half Dome from trail

in this area, resulting in some deaths. Fortunately, a safer route remains open during winter, allowing access to Nevada Fall, Little Yosemite Valley, and points beyond.

As in many trips originating in the Valley, you have to hike up to the snow line before donning your snowshoes. However, in average winters you shouldn't have to travel too far up the canyon before they become necessary. Most of the climb is quite steep. Only when you reach Little Yosemite Valley does the terrain mellow. In general, routefinding in the canyon is straightforward, but following every switchback and nuance in the trail when it's snow-covered is not a piece of cake. The precipitous climb coupled with the difficult terrain makes this trip one for experienced parties only.

For those interested in trips lasting more than a day, the backcountry of Little Yosemite Valley and beyond is boundless with opportunities. The campgrounds that backpackers use in the summer for climbs of Half Dome or trips to Tuolumne Meadow, make ideal basecamps for snowshoers on longer journeys into the Yosemite Wilderness.

Trailhead: Either follow directions in Trip 9 to the Day-Use Parking area or take the free shuttle bus to stop #14, Day-Use Parking/Curry Village.

Description: Begin your trip by walking the closed road ¾ mile up to Happy Isles. Cross the Happy Isles bridge to the east side of the Merced River and follow the wide path up to the official trailhead for both the John Muir and Mist trails. A large sign with numerous destinations and mileages greets you at the beginning of the trail. A smaller sign with map indicates the closed and the open portions of trails during the winter months.

Follow the route of the trail as you climb steeply up the Merced River canyon through light forest of evergreen and deciduous trees and past large granite boulders. As you progress up the trail, the steep cleft of Illilouette Gorge appears across the precipitous canyon. You continue to climb steeply until a sudden drop leads to the Vernal Fall Bridge, 1.6 miles from the bus stop. From the bridge you have a pleasant view of the fall up the canyon. A restroom building is located just over the bridge.

Not far from the Vernal Fall Bridge, you reach the junction between the Mist and John Muir trails. As the Mist Trail is closed during winter, turn sharply up the Muir Trail and begin a series of switchbacks up the steep hillside that culminate in Panorama Cliff. In the midst of the switchbacks, thanks in part to the leafless trees of winter, you have fine views of the canyon and Yosemite Falls. More switchbacks lead to the open rock slopes of Clark Point, 3 miles from the bus stop, where you have dramatic views of Nevada Fall, Liberty Cap, Mt. Broderick, and Half Dome. Nearby is the junction between the closed section of the Muir Trail and a lateral connection to the Mist Trail.

Descend from Clark Point for ½ mile via some more switchbacks to a junction with the Mist Trail. At the junction, you turn up canyon and follow the upper Mist Trail over a rock hump and across the footbridge over the Merced River. Once across the river, you follow the trail on a mild course through a moderate stand of cedars up alongside Nevada Fall. All too soon, the grade of the trail increases once more as you wind your way up the bottom of a steep gully. Half way up the gully, the trees are left behind and you proceed up through the narrow rock cleft via a series of tight switchbacks. The route straightens for a spell until another series of short switchbacks take you out of the gully to a trail junction, 4 ½ miles from the bus stop. From this junction, a short lateral trail heads off to the right to the top of Nevada Fall.

Beyond the junction, you follow the trail as it continues a winding climb, but at a much more pleasant grade. Traveling through light shrubs and scattered pines, you have glimpses of Half Dome, Quarter Domes and Clouds Rest before dropping down to the mild terrain of Little Yosemite Valley.

After all the steep climbing, snowshoeing on the nearly level floor of the valley is a real delight. As you progress up the valley, you follow alongside the Merced River, the lazy stream presenting a stark contrast to the tumultuous torrent of the lower canyon. Passing through moderate forest, you can roam up the valley as far as you like. The John Muir Trail northward and the Merced Lake Trail eastward offer a number of possibilities for lengthier journeys, and the popular Little Yosemite Valley Campgrounds make a fine basecamp for those wishing to extend their wanderings for overnight or multiday stays. However, the restroom is locked during winter, and the ranger station is unmanned.

Whatever your plans, leave enough time to complete your return before dark. Descending the steep route back down the canyon is to be avoided after nightfall at all costs.

FYI: To camp in Little Yosemite Valley, you must obtain a wilderness permit.

Warm-ups: Generally speaking, the cafeteria at Yosemite Lodge was created for those who eat to live as opposed to those who live to eat. However, the Coffee Corner is an oasis in the midst of this vast culinary wasteland. Open between the essential caffeine intake hours of 6:30 A.M. to 4:30 P.M., congenial coffee purveyors agreeably distribute their wide variety of lattes, mochas and espressos in every form short of an IV. If all you want is just a regular cup of joe, they have that too. While it may not be exactly like the Starbucks to which you've grown accustomed, can any one of their ubiquitous franchises boast a view of Yosemite Falls from outside their front door?

Trip 14

INSPIRATION POINT

Duration: ½ day
Distance: 2 ½ miles round trip
Difficulty: Moderate
Elevation: 4380/5365
Maps: 11; *El Capitan* 7.5' quadrangle, 1990
   Topographic Map of Yosemite Valley 1:24,000 scale, published by
   Wilderness Press, 1993

Introduction: A short but very steep climb leads you to Inspiration Point, the original first view of the valley for travelers along the old Wawona wagon road. The vista is not quite the same, thanks to the increase in vegetation over the years, but snowshoers can still find some excellent views nearby, 2500 feet above the valley floor. Many of the Park's most notable features can be seen, including Bridalveil Falls, El Capitan, Cathedral Rocks and Half Dome.

Even during the summer months, the steep nature of the climb is enough to discourage most people. In winter, snow blanketing the ascent route should frighten away even more folks, so having Inspiration Point to yourself is a reasonable expectation. As with all trips originating in Yosemite Valley, snow conditions are variable. At times, you may have to pack your snowshoes for the first part of this trip. Since the route ascends the north-facing side of the Valley, chances are good for decent snow conditions during most winters.

Trailhead: On the Wawona Road, at the east end of the Wawona Tunnel, park in the south parking lot across from Discovery View.

Stanford Point Valley view

Discovery View is 1 ½ miles from the junction with the Southside Road at the lower end of Yosemite Valley, near Bridalveil Falls. Find the Pohono Trail at the west end of the lot.

Description: The Pohono Trail wastes no time in climbing the steep southern wall of the Valley, as you ascend a series of switchbacks away from the parking lot. Intermittent gaps in the scattered shrubs and light-to-moderate forest allow fine views of Bridalveil Falls, El Capitan, Half Dome and Yosemite Valley along the way. The trail zigzags up the slope at a moderately steep grade, crossing an abandoned road heading east toward Artist Point and Bridalveil Falls at the 0.6-mile mark. Built in 1875, this old road was the original wagon route that brought visitors to Yosemite until replaced by the current Wawona Road in 1933.

Beyond the road crossing, the trail continues the steep climb for another 0.6 mile of switchbacks to the Inspiration Point area. A pair of metal signs with cut-out letters is the only marker suggesting this site has some significance. The old road used to pass through here, providing visitors their first glimpse of Yosemite Valley, much in the same way that Discovery View, 1000 feet below, impresses modern travelers. In the intervening decades, incense cedars, ponderosa pines, and black oaks have all grown up to obstruct the once-magnificent view, making this vista anything but inspiring. However, all is not lost, as a short walk west from the trail, followed by a quick descent to the edge of some cliffs, takes you to a superb view of the Valley.

When you have had your fill of the scenery, retrace your steps back to the Discovery View parking lot.

FYI: For even better views check out Trip 15.

Warm-ups: The ice-skating rink in Curry Village is open during the height of winter, usually from mid-November to early March, as weather permits. If you still need a little more recreation after a day of snowshoeing, the rink provides a fun way to burn up any remaining energy. Admission is $5.00 for adults and $4.50 for children. Rental skates are available for $2.00 per session. During the week, hours are noon to 2:30 P.M., 3:30 to 6:00 P.M., and 7:00 to 9:30 P.M. On weekends and holidays the rink hours are the same, with the addition of an 8:30 to 11:00 A.M. session.

While most all of the food services are closed at Curry during the winter, the pizza concession is usually open in the evenings from 5:00 to 9:00 P.M.

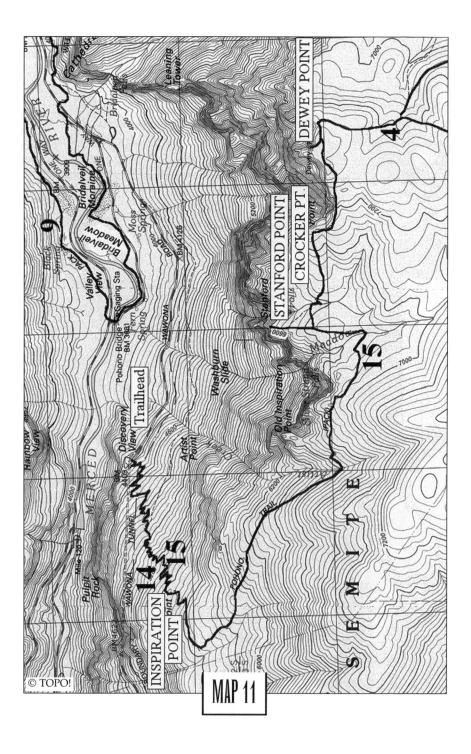

MAP 11

STANFORD POINT

Duration: Full day
Distance: 8 miles round trip
Difficulty: Difficult
Elevation: 4380/6950/6535
Maps: 11; *El Capitan* 7.5' quadrangle, 1990
        Topographic Map of Yosemite Valley 1:24,000 scale, published by
        Wilderness Press, 1993

Introduction: The vista from the edge of Stanford Point is one of the many spectacular panoramas seen from a variety of locations around the rim of Yosemite Valley. Most of these viewpoints are inaccessible in winter, or at least not without a supreme effort by skiers or snowshoers, some requiring multi-day journeys. By far the easiest, and most popular, route to a great view from the Valley rim is the winter route to Dewey Point (see Trip 4). Hundreds of cross-country skiers and snowshoers head to Dewey Point for the incredible scenery each sunny weekend day. In comparison, hardly anyone accepts the rigors of the steep climb from Discovery View to Stanford Point.

    Impractical for skis, the zigzagging Pohono Trail climbs over 2500 feet in 3 ¼ miles from the parking lot before dropping slightly over another ¾ mile to Stanford Point. The rugged ascent should be attempted only by snowshoers in good condition. The unmarked trail also requires a certain amount of routefinding skill, especially in following the snow-covered route of the summer hiking trail through light-to-moderate forest. Diligent snowshoers willing to not only

109

make the climb, but also to find their way, will be rewarded by solitude as well as the awe-inspiring view from Stanford Point.

At the viewpoint, Bridalveil Falls, Leaning Tower, El Capitan, Cathedral Rocks and a variety of other Yosemite landmarks make their appearance. Standing above the valley floor nearly 3000 feet below creates an overwhelming sensation as you survey the great expanse of the deep chasm. For additional views and further trip extensions, see FYI below.

Trailhead: Follow directions in Trip 14.

Description: Follow directions in Trip 14 to Inspiration Point.

From Inspiration Point, you continue straight up the hillside on a moderately steep climb incorporating a couple of switchbacks. After a couple of more bends, the route heads straight up the hillside once more. You continue the ascent through light forest for quite a distance until another pair of switchbacks zigzag across the slope. Cross a small creek and then begin a moderately steep climb across a face of the hill that lasts for a considerable distance. Just before you reach Artist Creek, the angle of the hillside grows steeper, making the traverse across the slope the most difficult part of the trip. Wrap around into the drainage and make a brief ascent up to the crossing of Artist Creek, 2 ¾ miles from the parking lot.

From the creek, you make a very brief, mild descent before resuming the climb out of the drainage. Head straight across the hillside and then turn sharply uphill to veer over the promontory ahead. As you continue the climb, through the trees to the north, you can identify the rocks of Old Inspiration Point. Approaching the top of the hill, trees become scattered and views begin to show some promise after the viewless climb from Inspiration Point. At the crest, 3 ¼ mile from the parking lot, the view is quite dramatic. Immediately ahead is the northward extension of Stanford Point protruding into the deep chasm of Yosemite Valley. If temperatures are warm enough, you may catch a glimpse of Silver Strand Falls spilling into the Valley from the cleft below Stanford Point.

Now you drop steeply down the hill to a crossing of Meadow Brook and then make a quick climb out of the drainage. Turn north and follow the gently sloping terrain down to Stanford Point, 4 miles from your starting point at Discovery View. As expected, the view from Stanford Point is spectacular. Notable landmarks visible from the overlook include Bridalveil Falls, Leaning Tower, Cathedral Rocks, El Capitan and Ribbon Fall.

FYI: If you still have time and energy after the trip to Stanford Point, the view from Crocker Point is even more spectacular. The price of that scenery is 400 feet of elevation gain and an additional ½ mile one-way to the point. The grander view includes more Valley landmarks as well as high peaks in the upper reaches of the Park.

An even more adventurous journey would be to travel all the way to scenic Dewey Point and then out to Badger Pass via one of the marked winter trails (See Trip 4). That route covers a total distance of 8 ¾ miles and requires a car shuttle or pick-up at Badger Pass. If you plan your trip for late winter or early spring, make sure the road to Badger Pass is still open before you set out. Otherwise you will have to walk an additional 5 miles down to the Wawona Road junction at Chinquapin.

Overnighters may consider reversing the route, beginning at Badger Pass and descending to Discovery View. This eliminates carrying a full pack up the steep route at the beginning of the trip. Remember, all overnight users must secure a wilderness permit.

Warm-ups: Each Wednesday night during the winter of '98-'99, Curry Village sponsored the Camp Curry Ski Buffet & Dance. A modest price of $12 for adults and $5 for children purchased a meal including choice of entree, assorted salads, vegetable and dessert. Dinner was served between 6 and 8 P.M., followed by dancing from 8 to 10 P.M.

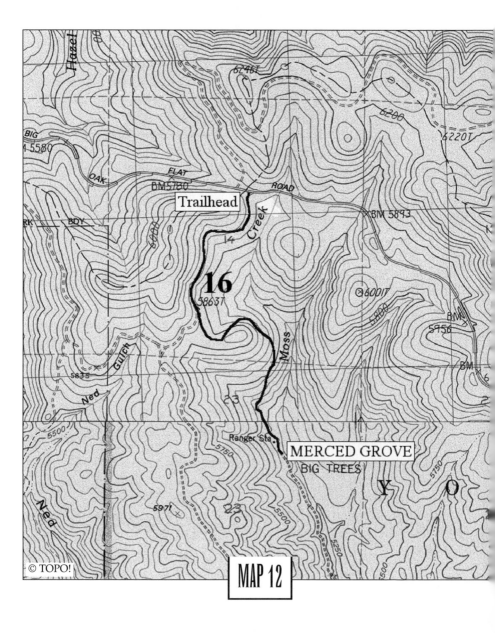

Trailhead

16
58637

MERCED GROVE
BIG TREES

Ranger Sta.

© TOPO!

MAP 12

MERCED GROVE

Duration: ½ day
Distance: 3 miles round trip
Difficulty: Easy
Elevation: 5840/5400
Maps: 12; *Ackerson Mountain* 7.5' quadrangle, 1990

Introduction: While the Merced Grove of giant sequoias is the smallest of the three groves in Yosemite, it is also the least frequented, affording winter visitors a chance of standing amid these giant trees without much human company. The route down to the grove is easy, both in length and in being all downhill. However, you must save enough energy to make the climb back up, especially the first mile, which is moderately steep.

Although the route has not been marked in the same fashion as the nearby Crane Flat winter trails, it is easy to discern, following a closed road all the way to the grove. The lower elevation dictates that you make this journey when snow cover is sufficient. By the beginning of spring, the road starts to shed its snow and the trip becomes more of a walk than a snowshoe.

Trailhead: Along Highway 120, find the small parking area for the Merced Grove on the south side of the highway. The turnoff is 7.3 miles east of the Big Oak Flat Entrance, or 3.5 miles west of the junction at Crane Flat.

113

Row of Giant Sequoias

Description: From the parking lot, follow the snow-covered road on a slightly descending grade through a mixed forest of cedar, pine and fir. As you head down the road, you will notice that the hill above on the right was the eastern limit of a recent fire. Follow this gentle route for a little over a half-mile, to a **Y**-junction.

At the junction, bear left, passing around a closed steel gate as the old road begins a more pronounced descent. Follow the road as it winds around and emerges into the drainage of Moss Creek, high above the tumbling stream. You continue to drop rather steeply as the road heads down toward the creek. Where the grade lessens, you encounter the first of the giant sequoias, a row of six stately trees, with a few more scattered around the hillside behind them.

You curve around while making a milder descent, reaching more sequoias about 100 yards farther down the road. At 1 ½ miles from the highway, you come to a cabin, which is staffed by a ranger in the warmer months. A few more big trees can be seen farther down the road.

After admiring the big trees, retrace your steps back to the parking lot. Obviously, the first mile of your journey back will be the most taxing part of your trip.

FYI: For a real adventure, you can extend your journey by continuing along the road past the grove, turning around wherever time and energy dictate. You could go all the way to Foresta if you desired. However, you would have to do some routefinding, as well as make arrangements for a pick-up at the far end.

Warm-ups: See Trips 9-15.

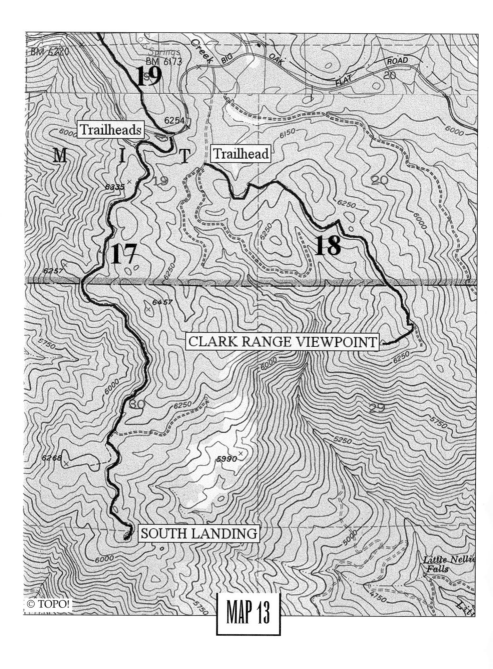

MAP 13

SOUTH LANDING

Duration: ½ day
Distance: 4 ¾ miles round trip
Difficulty: Moderate
Elevation: 6255/6345/6135
Maps: 13; *El Portal* 7.5' quadrangle, 1947 (photo revised 1981)
    Crane Flat Winter Trails map, 1986

Introduction: To escape the weekend crowds, the unmarked South Landing trip promises a modest opportunity for solitude. Even though the route is not marked in the same fashion as others in the Crane Flat network of trails, the road is easy to follow. The grade of the road is mild as well, demanding little climbing in either direction.

After cruising through light-to-medium forest cover for the first 2 miles, you break out into views of the Clark Range and the Merced Canyon near the end of the road. Here the lovely scenery combined with a sunny day makes for a fine lunch break or a relaxing rest stop.

Trailhead: On the Big Oak Flat Road (Highway 120), park on the shoulder 0.5 mile west of the junction with the Tioga Road at Crane Flat. This point is 6.8 miles east of the Big Oak Flat Entrance and 9.6 miles west of the junction with the El Portal Road (Highway 140).

The South Landing trip begins on the south shoulder opposite the starting point for the Crane Flat Lookout trip.

Description: Leave the Big Oak Flat Road and pass through an open steel gate, heading south on a snow-covered road through light, mixed forest. Continue along the road to a small flat, where you bend left. Winding through the trees of a medium forest cover, you proceed along the road, beginning a slight descent about ½ mile from the highway. One mile into your trip, the road passes above another flat, where a mysterious assortment of metal food storage boxes, picnic tables and fencing covers the area.

Rather than dropping into the flat, follow the road as it bends uphill to your left, crossing the Yosemite National Park boundary into the lands of Stanislaus National Forest. Follow the road on a slightly descending contour around the hillside through lighter forest cover. Although the trail is not marked in the same fashion as the Crane Flat Winter Trails, you do see a rash of orange markers just before reaching a junction near the ¾-mile mark. Ignore the lesser fork to your left (west) and remain on the main road to the right (south).

You crest a ridge and wrap around the hillside with the expectation of vistas ahead, and soon the Clark Range does pop into view, as well as a part of Merced Canyon. Continue to follow the road as you wind around, at or near the crest of the ridge, until a final climb leads to the top of the hill and the end of the road at South Landing. The best views actually occur below the high point, along a section of open road prior to the final climb.

FYI: If for some reason parking is not available at the trailhead, you can leave your car at the Crane Flat winter parking area and follow Crane Flat Winter Trail #7 southwest to the junction with Trail #6, and then south to the Big Oak Flat Road and the trailhead. However, such a diversion adds 2 miles to your round-trip total.

Warm-ups: See Trips 9-15.

CLARK RANGE VIEWPOINT

Duration: ½ day
Distance: 3 miles round trip
Difficulty: Moderate
Elevation: 6155/6455
Maps: 13; *Ackerson Mountain* 7.5' quadrangle, 1990
       Crane Flat Winter Trails

Introduction: To a great extent, experiencing Yosemite is about views. Most Valley visitors come to see the waterfalls, or the granite monoliths such as El Capitan or Half Dome, or the deep cleft of the Valley from Glacier Point. While the view from the climax of this trip isn't as notable as those, with a modicum of effort you can achieve a very pleasant panorama that most tourists won't see.

Most of this trip follows the nearly level grade of an old road on the way to a viewpoint at the end. Rather than follow the entire route of the road, this description makes a 200-ft. climb up a nearly bald hill for a much improved vista. The top makes for a pleasant lunch stop on a calm day, and chances are you won't have to wait for a table (see FYI).

Trailhead: From the Big Oak Flat Road (Highway 120), turn south 0.1 mile west of the junction with the Tioga Road, following signs for SNOW PLAY AREA, 7.2 miles east of the Big Oak Flat Entrance and 9.2 miles west of the junction with the El Portal Road (Highway 140). Drive down the road for 0.4 mile to the end and park as conditions allow. Find the beginning of Crane Flat Winter Trail #10 as marked by signs. Portable toilets are nearby.

Description: You start out snowshoeing the gentle road through mixed forest. Presently, you pass a trail junction with Crane Flat Winter Trail #11, which leads back to Crane Flat Campground. Continue to travel along the easy grade of the old road for 1 ¼ miles, until you come alongside a hill to your right. Find a convenient spot to leave the road and climb the steep slopes of the hillside through scattered trees to the top.

From the summit, you have a nice view of the surrounding topography. The prominent landmark to the east is the Clark Range, clad in a drape of white snow. Down below you have a bird's-eye view of the fire that swept through the forest some years ago adjacent to the Big Oak Flat Road.

FYI: You may not have to contend with a lot of company along this route. The view from the end of the road, which is the normal route as marked, is rather disappointing. By leaving the road and climbing to the top of the hill, not only do you improve the view tremendously, but you leave behind the few skiers who do use the trail.

Warm-ups: See Trips 9-15.

Clark Range Vista

CRANE FLAT LOOKOUT

Duration: ½ day
Distance: 3 miles round trip
Difficulty: Easy
Elevation: 6250/6645
Maps: 15; *Ackerson Mountain 7.5' quadrangle, 1990*
     Crane Flat Winter Trails

Introduction: The attraction of this trip is the easily obtained 360° view from the site of the Crane Flat Lookout. The route along marked Crane Flat Winter Trail #6, climbs at a relatively easy grade for most of the journey. At the lookout, a panorama of Yosemite National Park

Heading out

and the surrounding countryside greets you from atop the 6645-foot. mountain. Although forested terrain sprawls out in every direction from the lookout, the most notable landmark is the Clark Range to the east. Unlike many lookouts in this day and age, the one at Crane Flat is still manned during times of high fire danger.

Trailhead: Follow directions in Trip 17. The trailhead is on the north side of the highway, opposite the South Landing trailhead.

Description: Leave the highway and follow the snow-covered road on a moderately steep grade through scattered trees. The climb quickly abates where you enter more moderate forest cover. Follow a nearly level course which eventually becomes a more pronounced rise, reaching a junction with Crane Flat Winter Trail #7 near the ¾-mile mark.

Enjoying the view (Dewey Point trip 4)

Continue to climb mildly, until the grade abruptly increases as you near the hill upon which the lookout sits. As you climb up the slope, you will notice a restroom and a water tank to your right. A final climb leads to the lookout and the 360° view.

FYI: If parking spaces along the shoulder of the Big Oak Flat Road are not available, you can park at the Crane Flat winter parking area (see Trip 20) and follow Crane Flat Winter Trail #7 for ½ mile south and then west to the junction with this route.

Warm-ups: See Trips 7-12.

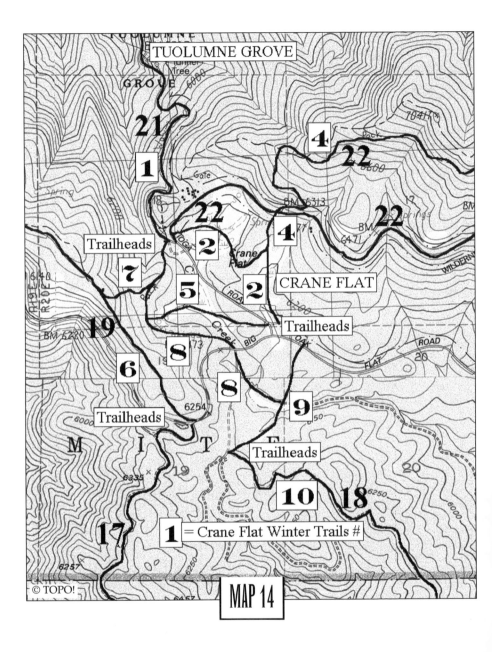

TUOLUMNE GROVE

MAP 14

1 = Crane Flat Winter Trails #

Trip 20

CRANE FLAT TRAILS

Duration: ½ day
Distance: Varies
Difficulty: Easy
Elevation: 6200
Maps: 14; *Ackerson Mountain 7.5' quadrangle, 1990*
       Crane Flat Winter Trails

Introduction: If you are new to the sport of snowshoeing, or if traveling with young children, Crane Flat has much to offer. A network of marked trails radiate from the winter parking area, providing plenty of opportunities for novices, big or small, to gain their "snow legs." Most of the shorter trails pass through the meadows of Crane Flat, making few demands on technique or routefinding.

Due to the ease of getting around on these trails, Crane Flat is a popular weekend destination. Most beginners don't mind the reassuring presence of crowds, but when you are ready to seek more of a backcountry experience, other trails in the area will provide more of a challenge. Not only will you find other snowshoers at Crane Flat, but a larger percentage of beginning cross-country skiers will most likely be present.

Trailhead: Drive on the Big Oak Flat Road to the junction at Crane Flat with the Tioga Road. This junction is 7.3 miles east of the Big Oak Flat Entrance and 9.1 miles west of the junction with the El Portal Road (Highway 140). Follow the Tioga Road (Highway 120) 0.6 mile to the Crane Flat winter parking area. Restrooms and a pay phone are nearby.

Description: Armed with a copy of *Crane Flat Winter Trails* a novice can find plenty of short, easy routes to follow around the meadows of Crane Flat. Routes 2 and 5, along with parts of routes 4, 7, 8 and the Tioga Road, can be combined to create brief loop trips requiring no considerable elevation gain or routefinding.

FYI: The service station at Crane Flat is open from 9:00 A.M. to 5:00 P.M., but you can purchase gas 24 hours a day with a credit or a debit card. You can also obtain a copy of *Crane Flat Winter Trails* for 50 cents. The station also has a limited supply of groceries.

Warm-ups: See Trips 9-15.

TUOLUMNE GROVE

Duration: ½ day
Distance: 2 ½ miles round trip
Difficulty: Easy
Elevation: 6200/5725
Maps: 15; *Ackerson Mountain* 7.5' quadrangle, 1990
   Crane Flat Winter Trails

Introduction: In days gone by, visitors could drive their vehicles down into the Tuolumne Grove of giant sequoias. As with the other two groves in Yosemite, the Park Service wisely discontinued this practice years ago. Now one must walk, ski or snowshoe the 1 ¼ miles to see these big trees. The journey into the grove is easy, as the road leads down the slope at a moderate grade. The return trip will be harder, but is not particularly difficult for anyone in reasonable shape.

Of the three groves in

Sign at Entrance to Tuolumne Grove

Tunnel Tree, Tuolumne Grove Trail

Yosemite, this is the most popular during winter. Don't expect solitude on a weekend of reasonable weather. If this route is too con-
gested for your taste, try Trip 16 to the Merced Grove instead.

Trailhead: Follow directions in Trip 20 to the Crane Flat winter parking area.

Description: From the parking area, head south past the restrooms
and find the closed gate at the beginning of the road leading down to

the Tuolumne Grove, corresponding to Crane Flat Winter Trail #1. Begin your trip with a slight descent through mixed forest of fir and cedar. Quickly the road makes a couple of sharp bends and then develops a more moderate rate of descent. Continue the decline around more curves, eventually reaching the signed entrance to the Tuolumne Grove, where the descent temporarily abates.

You continue down into the grove, encountering the first giant sequoias as you sweep around a hillside. A short lateral trail to the right leads to the Tunnel Tree, a sequoia with not only a hole in its base, but also a top resembling a tuning fork. The lateral trail loops back around to join the main road after a short distance. Wander around at your leisure, enjoying the 25 trees in the grove. Then climb back up the road to the trailhead.

FYI: For an interesting extension to your trip, consider continuing on the Old Big Oak Flat Road out past Hodgdon Meadow to the Big Oak Flat Entrance. The total distance is 6 ½ miles and is almost entirely downhill. You will have to arrange a pick-up at the entrance.

Warm-ups: See Trips 9-15.

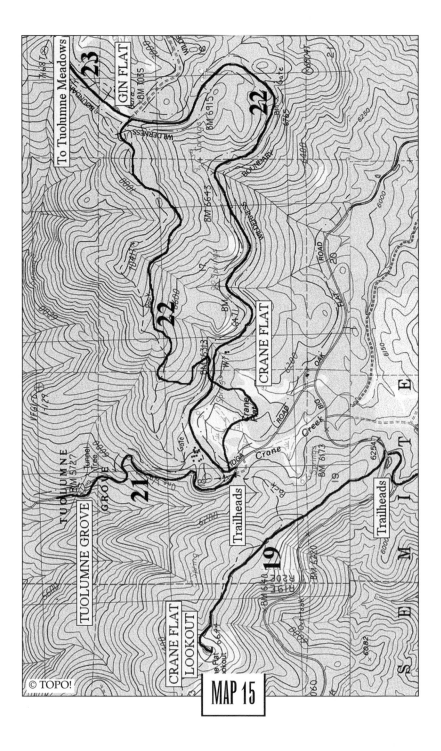

To Tuolumne Meadows

GIN FLAT

23

22

22

CRANE FLAT

TUOLUMNE GROVE

TUOLUMNE GROVE

21

Trailheads

Trailheads

19

CRANE FLAT LOOKOUT

YOSEMITE

© TOPO!

MAP 15

GIN FLAT LOOP

Duration: ¾ day
Distance: 6 miles loop trip
Difficulty: Moderate
Elevation: 6200/7080
Maps: 15; *Ackerson Mountain* 7.5' quadrangle, 1990
        Crane Flat Winter Trails

Introduction: A pleasant 6-mile loop takes snowshoers from the meadows of Crane Flat to those of Gin Flat and back again. Along the way you won't see many extraordinary landmarks, but the journey is quite pleasant as you wind your way through light and moderate forest. Since most of the Crane Flat Winter Trails are rather short in duration, this trip grants you the opportunity for a longer excursion. Following the Tioga Road for the first 3 miles, you are apt to see other skiers and snowshoers on weekends, but far fewer seem to follow Crane Flat Winter Trail #4 back toward the starting point.

Trailhead: Follow directions in Trip 20 to the Crane Flat winter parking area.

Description: From the parking area, you must walk the plowed but closed portion of the Tioga Road past the Yosemite Institute. Once you reach snow, travel along the Tioga Road, avoiding the ski tracks wherever possible. If you are here after a weekend and it has been a long while since any significant snowfall, the tracks may cover the road from one side to the other, as this route is extremely popular with cross-country skiers. Don't fear, just as long-distance runners start out in a big pack but quickly thin out, the number of tracks will diminish considerably after you put some distance between you and the trailhead. You continue to follow the road through light-to-moderate forest as it curves and bends on a nearly continuous climb. Reach the junction with Crane Flat Winter Trail #4, ½ mile from the parking lot. Trail #4 can be the route of most of your return.

As you progress up the Tioga Road, occasionally the trees will thin just enough to allow partial views of the distant ridges to the southeast. Otherwise the route up the road is uneventful. The miles tick by until you reach a 4-way intersection at the beginning of Gin Flat, 3 ¼ miles from the parking area. The Tioga Road continues straight ahead, tempting you with far-off destinations like Tuolumne Meadows and Tenaya Lake. The road to the right leads down to Tamarack Campground. Your route bends to the left and is signed: TRAIL 4, TIOGA ROAD.

You make a mild ascent along the Old Tioga Road for a short time before the beginning a mild descent. Entering back into moderate forest cover, the road gracefully curves through the trees as it cuts

Winter trail sign at Gin Flat

across a hillside. A long, straight stretch of moderate descent leads to more curves until a hairpin turn drops you back to a junction with the newer Tioga Road, at 5 ¼ miles from the parking lot. At the junction, you have two options. The first is to retrace your steps back down the Tioga Road to the parking lot. For more variety, option number two heads across the road following Crane Flat Winter Trail #4.

If you elect to follow Trail #4, after crossing the road you descend rather steeply through thick forest until the grade quickly levels and the forest begins to open. Soon you find yourself in one of the meadows of Crane Flat. Approximately ¼ mile from the road, keep your eyes open for the junction with Crane Flat Winter Trail #2 off to your right. After you locate the junction, follow Trail #2 across another portion of the meadow, briefly entering into light forest and then going back to the parking lot.

FYI: The area around Gin Flat makes a fine destination for an overnight stay. If you choose to camp here, you must have a valid wilderness permit. For a longer trip in the same area, consider a 2-mile extension to Tamarack Campground.

Warm-ups: See Trips 9-15.

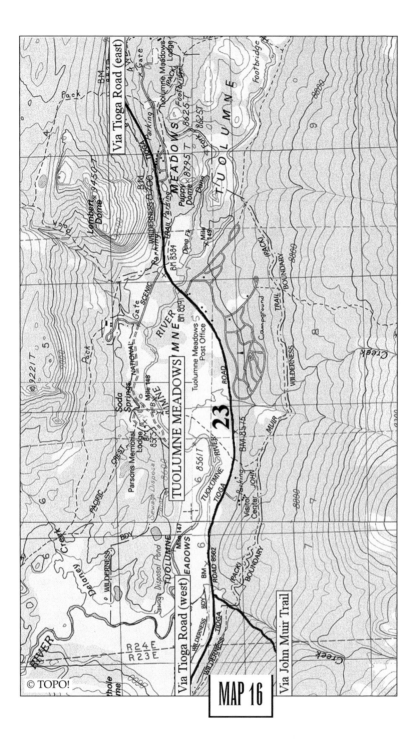

MAP 16

TUOLUMNE MEADOWS

Duration: Multi-day
Distance: Varies: 39 miles one way from Crane Flat via Tioga Road
    eastbound
    22 miles one way from Yosemite Valley via John Muir Trail
    16 miles one way from gate on Tioga Road westbound
Difficulty: Difficult to extreme
Elevation: 6200/8580 (Tioga Road eastbound)
    3980/8580 (John Muir Trail)
    7450/9945/8580 (Tioga Road westbound)
Maps: 16; *Ackerson Mountain, Tamarack Flat, Yosemite Falls, Tenaya
    Lake, Falls Ridge, Merced Peak* 1992 (provisional); *Vogelsang Peak
    & Tioga Pass* 1994 (provisional) 7.5' quadrangles

Introduction: Tuolumne Meadows is the Sierra's largest subalpine meadow. Thousands of visitors pass through the meadows each summer, but closed roads and the resulting lengthy approaches put this popular summer destination out of reach for tourists during the shortened days of winter. However, a growing number of outdoor enthusiasts come here each winter to ski, mountain climb, or snowshoe. For those willing to make the long journey, the area sparkles with majestic scenery and unparalleled beauty.

    The first choice prospective visitors must consider when contemplating a trip to the meadows is what route to travel. None of the options are easy, each one requiring a considerable investment in time and energy just to reach the meadows. From the west side of the mountains, the first of the two most logical choices are along the

135

Tioga Road, beginning at Crane Flat. The second option follows the route of the John Muir Trail. Of the two, the Tioga Road presents fewer routefinding difficulties, although the overall distance to Tuolumne Meadows is approximately 39 miles from Crane Flat. The trip along the John Muir Trail involves considerably more routefinding than the road, but is shorter at approximately 22 miles from Yosemite Valley.

From the east side, only one option exists. From a closed gate on the Tioga Road nearly 4 miles from US 395, travelers can continue up the steep section of Tioga Road, over Tioga Pass and then on to Tuolumne Meadows, a total distance of approximately 16 miles. For a fee, the folks at Tioga Pass Resort have been picking up and transporting the gear of skiers to their facility near the Saddlebag Lake junction, lightening the load for the 6-mile ski up the road to their facility. Unfortunately, the operators of Tioga Pass Resort have expressed a general disdain for snowshoers, so don't expect the same consideration if this option appeals to you.

Once at Tuolumne Meadows you can stay at the Park's Ski School Hut on a first-come, first-served basis. Even if you plan to stay there you should carry a tent and suitable overnight gear as there is no guarantee that you will be able to find space there. For guided trips you can contact the Yosemite Cross Country Ski Center and Ski School (see Appendix I).

A trip to Tuolumne Meadows is a serious multi-day undertaking that should be attempted only by those who are experienced in winter travel and in extended snow camping. Keep a close eye on the weather at all times and be prepared for all possibilities.

Trailhead: TIOGA ROAD EASTBOUND: Follow directions in Trip 18.
JOHN MUIR TRAIL: Follow directions in Trip 12.
TIOGA ROAD WESTBOUND: Follow directions in Trip 27. From the Ranger Station, continue up the Tioga Road to the closed gate, 3.7 miles from US 395.

Description: Tuolumne Meadows provides snowshoers with grand opportunities for wide-ranging explorations. The meadows themselves are quite extensive, granting those willing to go to all the trouble to get there a number of possibilities for exploration. Sprinkled with granite domes and resting in the shadow of high Sierra peaks, the meadows are worthy of as much attention as you can afford to give them. A more scenic winter landscape is hard to imagine.

From a base camp in Tuolumne Meadows, there are numerous creek drainages to trace, frozen lakes to find, and snow-covered peaks to climb. The only limitations to your explorations will be time and agreeable weather. Armed with the *Tioga Pass* and *Vogelsang Peak* quadrangles, outdoor adventurers can roam to their heart's content. The Tuolumne Meadows area has the potential for being the site of a great winter experience.

FYI: As for all overnight stays in the Yosemite backcountry, you need a wilderness permit. And for a journey of such proportions, a detailed description of your plans should be left with a reliable person back in civilization, complete with the phone number of the appropriate agency to contact if you don't return as scheduled.

Warm-ups: You're on your own for this one. Often when I plan a long trip into the backcountry, no matter what the season, I pack along something for a special occasion near the middle or end of the journey. Choose a favorite food or a hot drink that is a bit extravagant—at least by backcountry standards—tuck it in the recesses of your pack and bring it out for a treat when your party could use a lift. Tentbound days are greatly relieved by such pleasures.

CHAPTER 6

EASTERN SIERRA

The eastern escarpment of the High Sierra provides passers-by and recreationists with some of the most rugged and dramatic mountain scenery in the western United States. Precipitous slopes rise up steeply above adjoining valleys, culminating in airy peaks as high as 14,000 feet above sea level. Deep canyons periodically slice into these seemingly impenetrable walls, creating narrow gorges of access into extraordinarily scenic basins. With a bit of effort, snowshoers can sample some of this exquisite scenery and experience for themselves the majesty of the region.

Each summer, hordes of seasonal residents, sightseers, campers, anglers, hikers, backpackers and equestrians flock to the dancing streams, deep-blue lakes and flower-filled meadows. Mammoth Mountain and June Mountain ski areas aside, the conclusion of fishing season along with the first blanket of winter snow brings a halt to the hustle and bustle of activity along the east side of the central Sierra. Tourism-driven eastern Sierra communities, such as Bridgeport and Lee Vining, become virtual ghost towns after the last of the summer visitors retreat to warmer climates.

The season's first major snowfall typically closes Ebbetts,

Sonora and Tioga passes, thereby eliminating easy access to the east side of the range for millions of Californians. Once this occurs, those wishing to visit the region are forced to make long journeys from either southern or northern California, as there is no winter route across the Sierra for nearly 300 miles between Walker Pass on Highway 178 in the south and Carson Pass on Highway 88 in the north. Therefore, access to all eastside routes starts from US 395, the major north-south highway paralleling the crest of the range, aligned near the very base of the Sierra. Solitude-seekers will appreciate the handiwork of winter in eliminating passage to the recreation lands of the eastern Sierra.

Spanning the distance between Mammoth Lakes to the south and Sonora Pass to the north, the section of the central Sierra included in this guide possesses some incredible natural features. Even auto-bound visitors along the principal highway, US 395, are treated to superb views. Among the most notable highlights are vistas including the jagged Minarets rising triumphantly over the Mammoth Lakes region, uniquely austere Mono Lake, and serrated Sawtooth Ridge above Bridgeport Valley. Once snowshoers venture away from their cars, sheer mountains, glacier-carved canyons, frozen lakes, and eye-popping views are here for the asking.

However, the effects of winter are not all beneficial for recreationists searching for adventure in the glistening snow of the rain-shadow of the Sierra. Both access into areas of adequate snow cover and available parking are severely limited. Unless you are content to join the crowds at the downhill ski resorts or cross-country ski centers, finding decent snow at the beginning of trips and a parking spot to go along with it will be some of your most significant challenges. Variable road-plowing practices may create even more uncertainty in finding convenient places to park close to access points. In addition, many of the services provided in the small towns that dot the route along US 395 are substantially reduced during the winter months.

While most areas along the east side of the Sierra are lightly used in winter, there appears to be only two times of year when Mammoth Lakes even comes close to settling down after summer's flurry of activity. The first time occurs for a brief period in autumn, when light storms have sent most fair-weather visitors home and the

Robinson Creek Canyon

insufficient quantity of snow on the slopes has yet to attract the ski crowd. The only other relatively quiet period occurs a half year later, before snowmelt heralds the return of the summer crowd, and all but die-hards have grown weary of the lengthy ski season. On a smaller scale, the same seasonal fluctuations influence nearby June Lakes. If your desire for snowshoeing is to leave the crowds behind, make sure you avoid these two resort areas during the height of winter. Outside of these two areas, limited services can be obtained during the winter in the small towns of Lee Vining and Bridgeport.

These minor disadvantages aside, the eastern Sierra has much to offer the snowshoer willing to make the trek to this side of the range. As already mentioned, the dramatic topography is without parallel and the solitude rewarding. In addition, if the "Range of Light' can boast its incredible weather, then the eastern front of that range has even more reason to boast. Between storms, clear blue skies dominate the heavens, the imposing mountain chain of the Sierra Nevada acting as a barrier to much of the cloudiness moving in from the Pacific Ocean as well as blocking substantial amounts of the pollution created by industrial and metropolitan areas in the western valleys. Nothing can quite compare to the cobalt blue skies of winter from the high altitude of the eastern Sierra.

The steep hillsides and precipitous mountainous terrain certainly create many visual wonders throughout the eastern Sierra. However, one more caution is worth noting: under the right conditions these same picturesque slopes can be potentially dangerous when prone to avalanche. Always check the avalanche situation before embarking into suspect areas. When the snow is stable and the weather agreeable, the eastern Sierra rewards the outdoor adventurer with many outstanding possibilities.

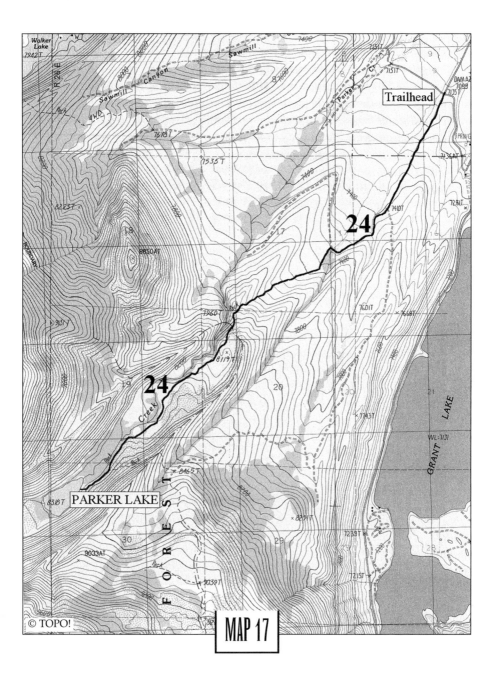

MAP 17

PARKER LAKE

Duration: Full day
Distance: 8 miles round trip
Difficulty: Moderate
Elevation: 7135/8320
Maps: 17; *Koip Peak* 7.5' quadrangle, 1994 (provisional)

Introduction: A moderate 4-mile climb leads to a pretty subalpine lake occupying a basin carved out at the very foot of the steep eastern face of the Sierra. The rugged terrain above the lake is unreachable as no trail escapes up the precipitous slopes surrounding the shoreline. The first part of the trip passes through typical eastern Sierra sagebrush country, before mountain mahogany and pines begin to appear near the halfway point. Once the trail joins Parker Creek, a series of meadows evidences a damper environment.
By the time you near the lake, a healthy forest of pine and aspen carpets the drainage.

On those rare occasions when snowfall creeps down the mountains and into the eastern valleys, access to this area may be temporarily cut off. However, the LA Water Department eventually will plow roads to access their diversion structures, if the snow refuses to melt on its own. At the very worst, you may have to add a mile or so to your journey if you can't get up the roads.

Trailhead: Follow directions in Trip 25 to the trailhead for Walker Lake. Continue on FS Road 1N17 for another 0.8 mile to a 4-way intersection. Park as near the intersection as conditions allow.

An alternate, if somewhat suspect, approach can be made from the south by heading up the north part of the June Lakes Loop, California Highway 158. In the winter, this road is usually gated one-third mile from US 395, but the gate is easily driven around on the wide gravel shoulder. The road is typically plowed for at least the next mile, from where you can turn onto FS Road 1S25 and access the intersection mentioned above, following road signs for PARKER LAKE ROAD and PARKER LAKE, WALKER LAKE. Travel up FS 1S25 for 0.4 mile to the intersection.

Description: Your trip begins as you follow the continuation of FS 1S25 as it climbs through open sagebrush slopes typical of the eastern Sierra. Continue to climb toward the looming east face of the mountains until a short descent interrupts the ascent just past the ½-mile mark. Resume the upward journey, passing a junction with FS Road 1S27 heading up the hillside to the south, at ¾ mile.

A mile from the intersection, the road bends and crosses a tributary of Parker Creek. The process is repeated in another third-mile as the road heads over the northern branch of the same stream. On the far side of the creek, you pass a road heading north as you follow

Parker Lake

the main road around to the east. You continue to climb along the road as it winds up through the sagebrush until it ends at the summer trailhead, 2 miles from the intersection.

Follow the trail as it climbs up through a swale, cresting near the Ansel Adams Wilderness boundary. Directly below you on the right, Parker Creek swings into view as you walk across the hillside high above the aspen-lined creek through scattered mountain mahogany and a few ponderosa pines. An angling traverse takes you across the steep hillside and out into an open meadow, where you have an excellent view of the peaks above the head of the canyon.

Beyond the meadow, you continue up the canyon on a mild course, passing through widely scattered pine and aspen. Above the steep canyon, Parker Creek assumes a gentler, meandering course as the trail draws near to the south bank and passes through some more meadows. Approximately a half mile from the lake, the forest thickens, forcing you to weave your way through aspens and pines. Continue to search for the most direct path and eventually you will arrive at the east shore of Parker Lake, 4 miles from the intersection.

Parker is a medium-sized lake, set in a deep canyon surrounded by steep slopes on three sides. The topography up the canyon is even more precipitous, evidenced by the fact that no trail exists beyond the lake. Except for the far shore, the lake is fringed by trees.

FYI: The name "Parker" appears on a handful of geographical features in and around the Mono Basin. Although no one is certain for which Parker they were named, careful inspection of the aspen grove ½ mile from Parker Lake reveals at least one tree with an inscription of *PARKER, 1846*.

Warm-ups: During the height of winter, Nicely's Cafe in Lee Vining is one of the few places to get a hot meal for many miles in either direction. This typical small-town cafe provides reasonable fare for breakfast, lunch and dinner every day but Wednesday.

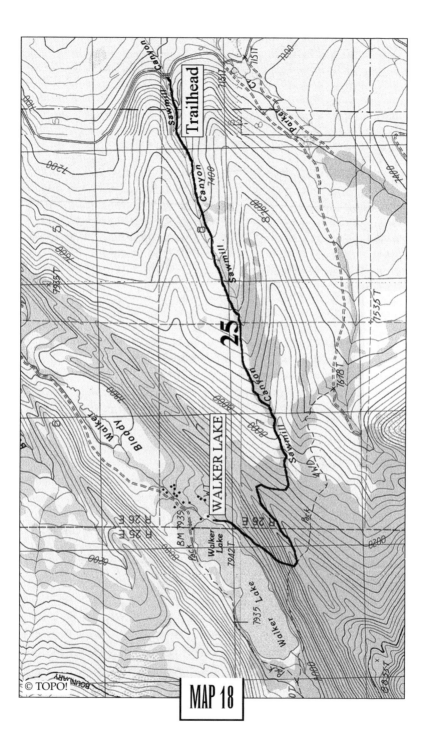

Trailhead

Sawmill Canyon

Canyon

Sawmill

25

Sawmill Canyon

Walker Blody

WALKER LAKE

R 26 E
R 25 E

Pack

BM 7935

Walker
Lake

7942T

7935 Lake

Walker Lake

4WD

Pack

R 26 E

© TOPO!

BOUNDARY

MAP 18

WALKER LAKE

Duration: Full day
Distance: 7 miles round trip
Difficulty: Moderate to difficult
Elevation: 7150/8450/7945
Maps: 18; *Koip Peak & Mt. Dana* 7.5' quadrangles, (provisional) 1994

Introduction: Providing you can drive your car all the way to the beginning of the road up Sawmill Canyon, this trip offers snowshoers a straightforward trip into the scenic basin of large Walker Lake. Three miles of relatively easy travel get you to the ridge above the lake, but the next half-mile down to the shore requires a precarious 500-foot descent on a steep hillside. Therefore, the trip to the ridge is rated moderate, while the route all the way to the lake has earned a difficult rating.

The trip begins in the wide-open vegetation typical of eastern Sierra approaches, allowing dramatic views of the peaks thousands of feet above. As you progress up Sawmill Canyon, pines, mountain mahogany and even some firs begin to welcome you into the range. Once at the lake, you will be blessed with superb views of the lake itself and the impressive ridges, slopes, and faces towering above the basin.

How to get there: From US 395, 2.5 miles north of the junction with Highway 120 East and 2.6 miles south of the junction with Highway 120 West, turn west onto FS Road 1N17, signed OIL PLANT ROAD. In all but the heaviest snowfall years, Los Angeles Department of Water and Power periodically plows this road to access their water diversion structures; otherwise you will have to snowshoe from the highway.

Drive, or snowshoe if necessary, 0.7 mile to the first junction and bear right (southeast). Bear left at 1.3 and again at 1.8 miles, where the other road is signed: BOWLER CANYON. Follow the road around a low hill to a **Y**-junction at 2.1 miles. Unless you're snowshoeing, ignore the temptation to follow this road up Walker Creek to Walker Lake, as this road is also only periodically plowed and has a locked gate ½ mile from the junction. If you left your car at the highway and have made it to this point on showshoes, follow this road 2 ¼ miles directly to the east end of the lake, as this will be your most direct route.

For those still behind the wheel, continue along Road 1N17 for another 1 ½ miles, 3.5 miles from US 395, to a junction with the road leading up Sawmill Canyon. A sign at this junction should read in part WALKER TRAIL with an arrow pointing up the westbound road. Park along the side of the road as conditions allow.

If an abundant snowpack prevents you from driving to the road up Sawmill Canyon, an alternate route from US 395 follows Forest Service Road 1N17 2 miles to the road heading directly up Walker Canyon to the lake. This alternate route will deliver you to Walker Lake in 4 ¼ miles, avoiding the steep descent of the standard route. Normal drawbacks to this route include a closed gate that blocks vehicle access, and only occasional road plowing to access the water diversion structure along Walker Creek.

Description: Begin a mild climb up the snow-covered road as you pass through open sagebrush terrain. The rugged eastern escarpment of the Sierra rises dramatically ahead. Approximately ¼ mile up the road, the grade increases near a grove of scattered pines on your left. Eventually, the forest becomes more pronounced as you continue to climb along the road. Cross the creek at 0.85 mile from Road 1N17.

After another 1 ¼ miles of steady climbing, the road bends north and climbs toward the ridge above the southeast shore of the lake. Along this traverse, periodically you have nice views of the Mono Craters to the east. One-fourth mile later, the road doubles back again and you have a grand view up the canyon toward Mono Pass, flanked by massive Mt. Gibbs to the north. Another ½ mile of nearly level travel brings you to the large parking area at the hikers' trailhead for the Walker trail, 3 miles from Road 1N17.

So far, the route along the road has been readily discernible and the snowshoeing fairly straightforward. The next part of your journey presents a greater degree of difficulty, as you must leave the parking area by making a quick climb to the crest of the ridge and then dropping precipitously across the steep face above the south shore of the lake. For those who wish to avoid the steep climb down to and back up from the lake, the view of the lake and canyon from the crest is quite impressive.

To reach the lake, the best route angles across the hillside toward the outlet. The upper part is the steepest section of the half-mile descent. Exercise caution as you drop to the lake, and make sure you have enough energy left to make the climb back up to the ridge. Nestled in the steep-sided canyon, the forest-rimmed lake lies serenely beneath the rugged eastern Sierra. From the shores of Walker Lake you have splendid views of the Mono Pass environs, dwarfed by the dramatic slopes of massive Mount Gibbs and Mount Lewis.

Road to Walker Lake

FYI: Extending your journey up the Bloody Canyon to the Sardine Lakes or the Mono Pass region is possible, but the terrain is steep and should be avoided during unstable snow conditions. Lower Sardine Lake is 2 miles and 2000 feet above Walker Lake.

Warm-ups: See Trip 24.

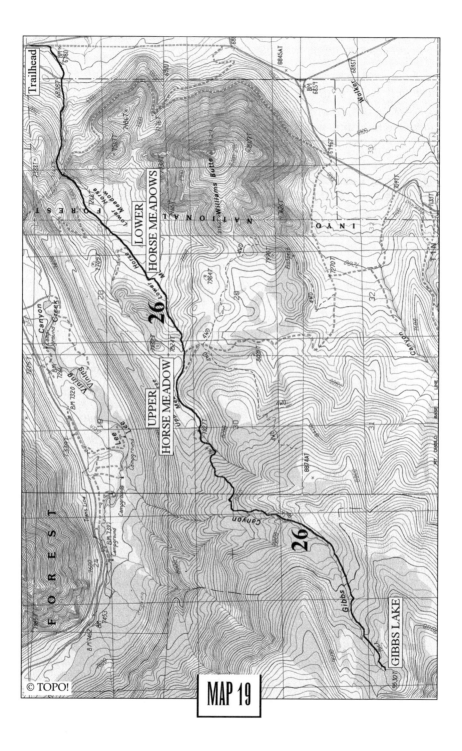

MAP 19

GIBBS LAKE

Duration: Full day
Distance: Varies—up to 12 ¼ miles round trip
Difficulty: Difficult
Elevation: 6775/9530
Maps: 19; *Lee Vining & Mt. Dana* 7.5' quadrangles (provisional), 1994

Introduction: A secluded, beautiful lake is the destination of this trip. Depending on snow conditions, the length of your journey can vary. During the height of winter, you may have to park along US 395 and snowshoe the full 6 miles to the lake. In light snow years, or in spring as the snow line creeps up the hillsides, you may be able to drive a significant distance up the road. Whatever the length of your trip, Gibbs Lake is a worthy goal, the rugged basin providing outstanding scenery below the massive peaks of Mt. Gibbs and Mt. Dana. If the snow is deep and you're looking for a shorter trip, Upper and Lower Horse Meadows are scenic destinations in their own right.

The first part of the journey past the meadows follows the clearly defined route of FS Road 1N16. To reach only Lower or Upper Horse Meadows, the trip rating is easy. Above the meadows, parts of the route are steep, and once you reach a point about ¾ mile beyond the summer trailhead, the road seems to disappear, making the routefinding more of a challenge. The last part of the journey follows alongside Gibbs Creek through moderate forest cover without many landmarks. Once you locate the creek, the route continues up the forested drainage to the lake.

151

Trailhead: On US 395, find the signed turnoff to HORSE MEADOWS 1.1 miles south of the junction with Highway 120 West (Tioga Road). If conditions allow, drive up the road until snow blocks your progress; otherwise park on the shoulder of US 395.

Description: From US 395, follow FS Road 1N16 as it heads toward the eastern front of the Sierra, passing through typical sagebrush-covered terrain. Follow the course of the road and reach a **Y**-junction at ¼ mile. Continue straight ahead at the junction, after which you enter a canyon as you travel above a small creek. At 1 mile, a road signed AQUEDUCT ROAD heads downhill to the left (southeast). You continue to wind through the canyon above the aspen-lined creek for a short distance, soon emerging into the lengthy expanse of Lower Horse Meadow at 1 ¼ miles. As you travel through the mile-long meadow, ignoring a pair of lesser roads to the right, you have continuous views of the eastern face of the Sierra, including 13,057-foot. Mt. Dana and 12,773-foot. Mt. Gibbs.

Mt. Gibbs

From the far end of the meadow, the road climbs moderately steeply through scattered pinyon pines. The grade where you reach Upper Horse Meadow, 3 miles from US 395. Travel along the edge of the meadow through a light grove of pines. The upper meadow is about half the size of its lower counterpart, and you reach the end at 3.5 miles. A short distance farther, you come to the end of the road and the beginning of the summer trail, where you may find an information board next to a closed gate across the road.

Now you climb steeply through scattered pine forest on a slightly winding ascent.

About ¾ mile from the summer trailhead, the grade eases as the trail bends south, climbing up through a low swale. Continue up the swale to the crest of a hill and then start to curve around to the east above Gibbs Creek through moderate forest cover. Continue to follow the stream on a westerly course through the trees. Eventually you reach the lake, just over 6 miles from the highway.

Gibbs Lake is situated at the very base of the precipitous cliffs rising up to Peak 12565. Hills on either side form the deep basin that cradles the lake. Scattered groves of fir and pine grace the area, a number of old weather-beaten trees adding character to the shoreline. The basin is truly a picturesque destination, aided by the view of towering Mt. Gibbs and Mt. Dana.

FYI: If you reach Gibbs Lake with both time and energy to spare, you can follow Gibbs Creek steeply up to the austere surroundings of Kidney Lake, an appropriately named body of water slightly larger than Gibbs.

Warm-ups: See Trip 24.

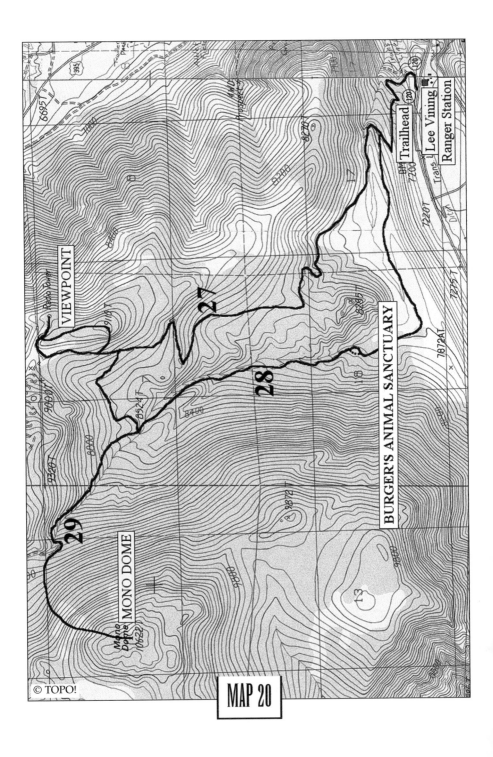

VIEWPOINT

BURGER'S ANIMAL SANCTUARY

MONO DOME

27

28

29

Trailhead

Lee Vining
Ranger Station

© TOPO!

MAP 20

Trip 27

MONO LAKE VIEWPOINT

Duration: ¾ day
Distance: 7 miles round trip
Difficulty: Moderate
Elevation: 7210/9110
Maps: 20; *Mount Dana* 7.5' quadrangle (provisional), 1994
　　　Hoover Wilderness, Toiyabe & Inyo National Forests, 1987

Introduction: Great views of Mono Lake and the central Sierra are the chief attractions of this trip, which follows an old road to the very edge of the eastern Sierra. Standing at the apex of the steep slope that rises 2600 precipitous feet from the shore in little over a mile, a finer vantage point from which to view the lake is hard to imagine. Another half mile from the view of Mono Lake is the climax of a ridge providing equally rewarding views of the eastern front of the Sierra. Thanks to the road, the routefinding is easy and the steady grade requires just a modicum of conditioning in order to reach the views.

Due to a location well east of the crest, you may find little or no snow at the beginning of the trip. You may have to walk up the road to reach the snow.

How to get there: From U.S. 395 just south of the town of Lee Vining, drive 1.2 miles westbound on the Tioga Road, Highway 120, to the right-hand turn onto Log Cabin Road. If conditions permit, you can drive a short distance up it to the snowline and park beside the road. Otherwise, when snow covers the surface, park in the Forest Service Ranger Station lot across the highway.

Description: From the junction with Highway 120, begin climbing up Log Cabin Road at a moderate grade through sagebrush-covered slopes dotted with pinyon pine. Very quickly you encounter a junction with a road to your right, where you should bear left and continue climbing up the winding course of the main road. As you ascend, alternately you have nice views of a part of Mono Lake, and of the striking east face of rugged Koip Crest, along with 13,057-foot Mt. Dana and 12,773-foot Mt. Gibbs. Two-thirds mile from the Tioga Road, you encounter a junction with a road to your left which heads toward Burger's Animal Sanctuary (see Trip 28). Bear right at this junction, pass through an open gate, and proceed up FS Road 1N03.

Just beyond the junction, you bend west and follow a creek for ¼ mile before turning northwest, 1.0 mile from the highway. The scarcity of trees in this section allows excellent views of the eastern Sierra, including Koip Crest, Mt. Dana, Mt. Gibbs, Mt. Lewis, June Mountain, and a host of other peaks along with Mono Basin and the Mono Craters to the east. Another ½ mile of travel along the road brings you to a series of S curves, where you enter a light forest of mountain mahogany, pinyon pine and ponderosa pine. Follow the winding road, continuing to climb amid cover of light forest.

Mono Lake from overlook

Eventually the road straightens and pursues a northerly course for a spell before reaching a trio of long switchbacks, which begin 2 ¼ mile from the Tioga Road. After the switchbacks, continue north along the road, passing below a rocky hill and heading toward a saddle in the crest ahead. Nearly 3 ½ miles from the start of your trip, you encounter a **Y**-junction, where a lesser road curves east. Follow this lesser road to the crest of the ridge, from where you have an incredible, unobstructed view of Mono Lake, 2600 feet directly below. The dramatic plunge in elevation occurs in the span of a mile, creating a veritable nightmare for vertigo sufferers. Watching the subtle interplay of transforming hues on the mysterious lake against the backdrop of the Great Basin sky can be a truly rewarding experience.

Once you have sufficiently sampled the views of Mono Lake from the saddle, you should head along the ridge to the high point, one-third mile south. From this apex the eastern escarpment of the central Sierra spreads out like the leading wave of a white-capped sea poised to crash upon the eastern valleys. Peaks are almost too numerous to count—be sure to bring a map large enough to help you identify them. Among the more notable mountains visible from this perch are Mt. Lyell, Banner Peak, Mt. Ritter, the Minarets, Mammoth Mountain and Mt. Morrison.

If you don't mind the steep slope and a zigzagging route through mountain mahogany, descending directly from the high point back to the road is possible, rather than returning via the saddle.

FYI: For more variety on your return, connect with the road that passes through Burger's Sanctuary. From the viewpoint, follow your steps back along the road to an area just south of and below the rocky high point. Look for an obscure junction with a road heading west and follow it ½ mile to the more obvious road paralleling the creek Don't worry if you can't make out the path of the road—just head downhill to the west, headed for the creek. Once you find the road, turn southeast, reversing the description in Trips 28 and 29.

Warm-ups: See Trip 24.

Trip 28

BURGER'S ANIMAL SANCTUARY

Duration: ¾ day
Distance: 6 miles round trip
Difficulty: Moderate
Elevation: 7210/8550
Maps: 20; *Mount Dana* 7.5' quadrangle (provisional), 1994
  Hoover Wilderness, Toiyabe Inyo National Forests, 1987

Introduction: This trip offers a pleasant stroll through a variety of eastern Sierra environments. Whether you desire great views of the rugged eastern Sierra across open sagebrush slopes, extensive aspen groves, or the lush vegetation along a picturesque creek, the trip to Burger's Animal Sanctuary has these and more. The route follows the well-defined course of a road for the entire journey, making routefinding a cinch. The grade of ascent is reasonably easy as well.

Chances are you will have the area to yourself on most winter days. The forested environment along the second half of the trip seems to accentuate the feeling of solitude. With a location near the eastern edge of the Sierra, you may have to walk a short distance from your vehicle to get adequate snow cover, but odds are you won't have to go far.

Trailhead: Follow directions in Trip 27 to the trailhead across from the ranger station.

Description: Follow directions in Trip 27 to the road junction two-thirds mile from Highway 120.

Bear to the left (west) at the junction and follow the road on a moderate climb through sagebrush as it heads straight toward the eastern face of the Sierra. A series of signs notify you of your entry into Burger's Animal Sanctuary, providing information on the history of the area as well as prohibitions against hunting. The grade of ascent mellows out and soon you draw near to a willow-lined creek. At 1 ½ miles the road bends sharply to the north around a rock cliff, leaving the views of Mt. Gibbs, Mt. Dana and the Koip Crest behind.

After you follow the bend in the road, you enter an extensive grove of dense aspen. Named Robin's Grove, the trees form a very picturesque setting. Beyond the aspen grove, near the 2-mile mark, you encounter the varied cabins of Burger's Animal Sanctuary. The rustic resort has a number of buildings as well as signs indicating the type of flora and fauna that have been identified from the surrounding area. Pass through the resort with respect for the private property, and continue to head up the road passing through a medium forest of pine, fir and aspen.

The road parallels the lushly vegetated creek as it makes a mild-to-moderate climb. Above the creek, the hillsides are covered with a smattering of mountain mahogany, pinyon pine and ponderosa pine. As you continue up the road, you eventually reach an old dam across the creek built in the early Sixties for who knows what purpose. Shortly beyond the dam, the road crosses the creek.

The route description ends at this point, but options are many for extending your trip (see FYI).

FYI: By heading northeast for ½ mile, you can make a connection with the road to the Mono Lake viewpoint and loop back to the car (see Trip 27). Continuing farther up the road for quite a distance to a Boy Scout Camp or the site of an old mine is also a possibility. For a climb of nearby Mono Dome, see Trip 29.

Warm-ups: See Trip 24.

Trip 29

MONO DOME

Duration: Full day
Distance: 9 ¾ miles round trip
Difficulty: Difficult
Elevation: 7210/10622
Maps: 20; *Mount Dana* 7.5' quadrangle (provisional), 1994
      Hoover Wilderness, Toiyabe & Inyo National Forests, 1987

Introduction: For an awe-inspiring view, the climb to Mono Dome will not disappoint you. The eastern face of the Sierra is seemingly close enough to reach out and touch. The dramatic peaks surrounding the Tioga Pass region fill the western horizon, while the lofty peaks along the eastern front line up in a continuous parade to the south.

The slopes of Mono Dome are steep and should be attempted only by those with advanced skills. In addition, the rainshadow effect on this area can create difficult snow conditions from time to time.

Trailhead: Follow directions in Trip 27 to the trailhead across from the ranger station.

Description: Follow directions in Trip 28 to the end of the description.

Continue to climb along the road as it parallels the creek. Just after a pair of sharp bends in the road, near the 4-mile mark, find a convenient place from which to leave the road and climb the steeper

160

slopes on the northeast face of Mono Dome. Climb west toward the ridge and then bear south to the summit.

FYI: As previously mentioned, the snow conditions around Mono Dome can be highly variable not only from season to season but within a single season as well. Check with a ranger at the Lee Vining Ranger Station on current snow conditions before departing on your journey.

Warm-ups: See Trip 24.

Mono Dome from road

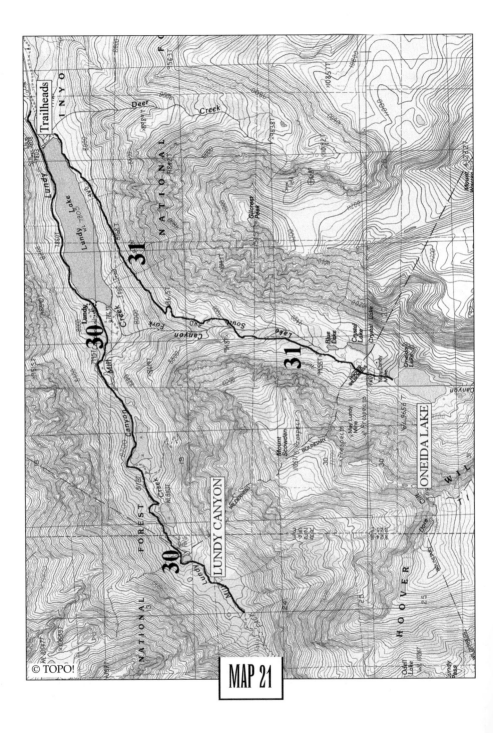

MAP 21

LUNDY CANYON

Duration: ¾ day
Distance: 8 ½ miles round trip
Difficulty: Moderate
Elevation: 7785/8600
Maps: 21; *Lundy & Dunderberg Peak* 7.5' quadrangles (provisional), 1994
   Hoover Wilderness, Toiyabe & Inyo National Forests, 1987

Introduction: Lundy Canyon offers snowshoers the opportunity to experience the spectacular scenery of an eastside Sierra canyon with a modicum of effort. The route gains less than 1000 feet in 4 ¼ miles and the routefinding on the old road and the hiking trail is straightforward. From all along the route you have superb views of the steep canyon walls and tall peaks over 11,000 feet. If you have to park at the end of the plowed road rather than at the gate, you will still be blessed with the extraordinary scenery, even if you can't get all the way to the head of the canyon.

As in most canyons slicing into the steep escarpment of the eastern Sierra, avalanches do occur in Lundy Canyon under the right conditions. Do not enter Lundy Canyon when avalanche conditions are unstable, as you would be a sitting duck for anything coming off the steep canyon walls.

Trailhead: Follow US 395 to the junction with Highway 167, 7 miles north of Lee Vining and 18 miles south of Bridgeport. Instead of turning east onto Highway 167, follow signs for Lundy Lake and turn west up the two-lane paved road. Cal Trans plows the first 1.4 miles of roadway but, if conditions allow, continue another 2.2 miles to the closed gate just short of Lundy Lake.

Description: If you had to park at the end of the plowed road, proceed up the road 2.2 miles to the gate. From the gate, you climb up the road ¼ mile to the east side of Lundy Lake. Follow the road on a level grade above the north shore for the next 1 ¼ mile to the west end of the lake. While traveling along the road, you have an excellent view of the impressive east face of Mt. Scowden above Lake Canyon (see Trip 24).

At the far end of the lake, pass through Lundy Lake Resort, which offers summer visitors a wide array of amenities but is closed in winter. As you stroll past the general store and cabins, remember to show respect for the property rights of the resort owner by staying on the road. A short climb leads away from the resort until the grade eases as you draw near to the creek. You pass some beaver ponds and soon reach the end of the road and the site of the Lundy Canyon trailhead.

From the summer trailhead, continue up the canyon on a mild grade, passing through extensive stands of aspen. As you approach the next beaver pond, you must decide how you will surmount the wall at the far end, where a waterfall spills down a nearly vertical face. The hiking trail makes a winding climb above the cliffs to the right of the pond, and this will be the easiest route for snowshoers if there is not much snow in the canyon and you can discern the path. When ample snow covers the brush, you may be able to snowshoe around the right side of the lake below the fall and ascend the steep wall just to the right of the waterfall.

Whichever way you choose to ascend the wall, your route above it follows alongside the creek before veering away momentarily to cross a pair of side streams coming down from the north. Continue up the canyon past another beaver pond and pass through a light forest of aspen, pine and fir.

Eventually you break out into the open again in the upper part of the canyon. As you peer at the nearly 2000-foot-high canyon walls, a way up and out of this chasm seems impossible, but a hiking trail does snake up the south side near the creek which drains from Lake Helen. The level floor of the basin near the head of the canyon is wide open, sprinkled with dwarfed pines, low-growing aspens, and brush, and is well-suited for exploration. At the conclusion of your wanderings, retrace your tracks to your vehicle.

FYI: For those who are extremely experienced in backcountry travel, zigzagging up the course of the hiking trail out of the canyon and up to the secluded lakes basin above is possible—an incomparable overnight adventure. However, an easier route extends north from Saddlebag Lake.

Warm-ups: Options for enjoying food or beverage are very limited along the east side of the Sierra during the winter. However, 75-year old Mono Inn, on US 395 just 3 miles south of the junction with the Lundy Canyon Road, is open for dinner during the winter on Thursday through Sunday evenings. Owned and operated by a granddaughter of famed photographer Ansel Adams, the recently remodeled Inn houses an Ansel Adams Gallery on the main floor and an upscale restaurant below. The restaurant ambiance is elegant, views of Mono Lake through tableside picture windows incredible, and the food superb. Prices for entrees begin at $15. Although the staff was very welcoming to a pair of disheveled snowshoers, we would have felt more at ease in the posh surroundings after a shower and a change of clothes.

Trip 31

LUNDY CANYON TO ONEIDA LAKE

Duration: ¾ day
Distance: 7 ½ miles round trip (12 miles from end of plowed road)
Difficulty: Moderate
Elevation: 7785/9655
Maps: 21; *Lundy & Dunderberg Peak* 7.5' quadrangles, (provisional), 1994
   Hoover Wilderness, Toiyabe & Inyo National Forests, 1897

Introduction: Beautiful alpine scenery, high mountain lakes, and historical interest combine to make the trip into Lake Canyon a rich experience. If you don't mind the steady climb necessary to reach the upper canyon, the rewards are plentiful. Nestled into a narrow cleft below 1500-foot cliffs, four lakes beckon the adventurous snowshoer to experience their shores. The largest, Oneida Lake, is one of the prettiest lakes you will find in the area.

For historical appeal, the area around Crystal Lake is replete with mining artifacts and structures from the days of the May Lundy Mine. A light snowpack enables those interested in the bygone days of mining in the eastern Sierra an opportunity to explore the once-bustling district.

Bent and broken trees on the hillsides of Lake Canyon tell us that avalanches have roared down the steep slopes and across the floor of the basin. Proceed into the area only when the snow is stable, and exercise caution.

Trailhead: Follow directions in Trip 30 to Lundy Canyon. Park at the end of the plowed road, or if conditions allow, continue another 2.1 miles to the Lundy Dam Road. Turn left and follow the gravel road 0.3 mile down to a parking area near the dam, where a steel gate blocks travel farther up the road.

Description: If you had to park at the end of the plowed road, snow-shoe up the Lundy Canyon Road to the Lundy Dam Road, and then drop down to the dam. From the gate, follow the single-track mining road just above the south side of Lundy Lake through young aspens at the base of a steep hill covered with sagebrush. About ¼ mile from the dam, the road begins to climb across the hill at a moderate grade. As you ascend, the rugged north face of Mt. Scowden is constantly in view. Continue to ascend this road at a steady rate for 1 ¼ miles until you reach a pair of short switchbacks, after which the road bends south to proceed up Lake Canyon.

The steady climb continues as you head up the canyon directly below the north face of Mt. Scowden. Pass through a grove of lodge-pole pine and then make a slight descent to a crossing of the South Fork Mill Creek, 2 ¼ miles from the dam. Once you cross the creek,

Oneida Lake

the moderate ascent resumes as the terrain alternates between open areas and more groves of pine. Just where the road levels out, the trees thin and you pass 50 yards to the right of the first frozen body of water in Lake Canyon, Blue Lake, a rather uninteresting little lake that occupies an open basin near the bottom of steep canyon walls.

A short distance beyond Blue Lake you encounter a Y in the road. The main road heads to the right, while the left branch leads over to Crystal Lake. Although narrow Crystal Lake is enclosed by dramatic cliffs, the most interesting feature is not the scenery but the plethora of mining equipment and structures scattered around the basin. Rock walls, twin 25-foot-diameter tubs, ore cars, buildings, and pieces of equipment too numerous to list are strewn around the lakeshore and up the hillsides. The original May Lundy Mine was established by William O. Lundy around 1880 and was named after

Snowshoeing in Lakes Canyon

his daughter. If the snowpack is light, you should be able to spend hours exploring the remains.

Back on the main road, you make a short climb up past a pile of tailings to the actual mine. A set of tracks still lead back into the old, boarded-up shaft. The path beyond the mine becomes less distinct, but you should have no trouble making the short jaunt over to the largest and prettiest of the lakes in the canyon, Oneida Lake.

Surrounded by a scattered forest of pine and fir, Oneida Lake is very picturesque. The serenity of the lake overshadows the intrusiveness of the mine just ¼ mile behind you. Just inside the Hoover Wilderness boundary, Oneida Lake seems worlds apart from the previous two lakes. Rolling terrain beyond the far shore culminates in the steep canyon walls of the Tioga Crest at the head of the gorge, forming an exquisite backdrop to the frozen expanse of the lake.

If you still have time and energy, you can continue another ¾ mile to the last lake in the chain, at the very head of Lake Canyon. Finally, retrace your steps back to the trailhead at Lundy Dam.

FYI: In spite of the evidence of extensive mining activity in the basin, you still may be surprised to see another shaft with a wooden structure perched high up the slopes of Gilcrest Peak on the east side of the canyon. It would take a steep, long climb to reach the site.

Warm-ups: See Trip 30.

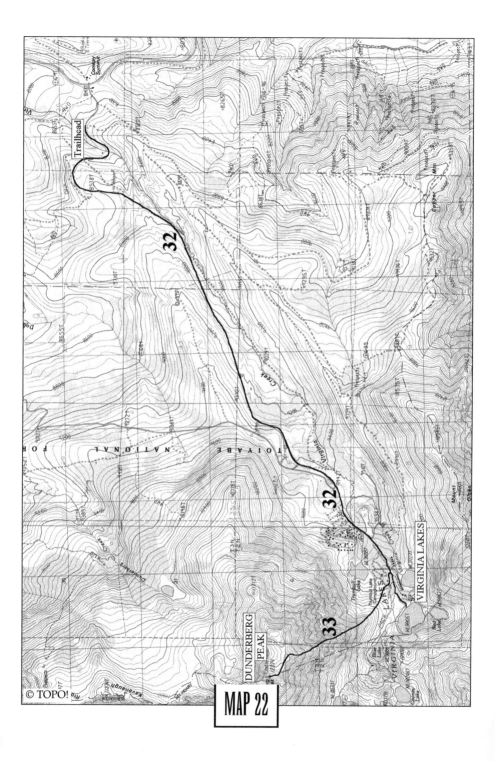

Trailhead

32

32

33

DUNDERBERG PEAK

VIRGINIA LAKES

© TOPO!

MAP 22

Trip 32

VIRGINIA LAKES

Duration: Full day
Distance: 11 ½ miles round trip
Difficulty: Moderate
Elevation: 8260/9780
Maps: 22; *Lundy & Dunderberg Peaks* 7.5' quadrangles, (provisional), 1994
    Hoover Wilderness, Toiyabe & Inyo National Forests, 1987

Introduction: The trip into Virginia Lakes begins at one of the very few plowed parking areas on the east side of the Sierra. The journey takes you on a steady climb along a road to a group of frozen lakes. The scenery along the way is quite pleasant, as the road passes through open terrain with wide-ranging views of the eastern Sierra. At the lakes, the visual pleasures continue as you experience the picturesque lakes with the dramatic backdrops of Dunderberg Peak and Black Mountain.

Because of the open nature of the terrain and the elevation, the trip into Virginia Lakes should be avoided when foul weather kicks up strong winds. Most of the route is quite exposed, providing little shelter from blustery conditions. Otherwise, if it wasn't for the 5 ¾ mile distance, the trip would be rated as easy, since the route follows a road for the entire trip, requiring little routefinding.

If you're looking for an area on the east side of the Sierra for an overnight or a multi-day trip, the Virginia Lakes offer plenty of additional possibilities for extending your wanderings (see FYI below).

Trailhead: Drive to Conway Summit and turn west onto the Virginia Lakes Road. This junction is 13 miles south of Bridgeport and 12 miles north of Lee Vining. Follow Virginia Lakes Road 0.4 mile to the cleared winter parking area.

Mono County usually begins to plow the road into Virginia Lakes in early spring, allowing late-season snowshoers and skiers the possibility of extending their wanderings farther up the canyon.

Description: You climb away from the parking area, following the snow-covered road on a moderate grade. After ¼ mile, the grade increases as the road begins a bend around a low hill. For a while you have nice views east across Bridgeport Valley to the Sweetwater Mountains. As you loop around and head southwest, some of the Sierra peaks pop into view, Dunderberg Peak, the most notable summit, being directly west. You continue the steady climb, passing through typical eastside Sierra vegetation—predominantly sagebrush-covered slopes with widely scattered pines and a few isolated groves of aspen.

Views to the south of the Sierra continue to improve as you climb. About 1 ½ miles from the trailhead, you draw near to Virginia Creek and continue the ascent quite a way above the north side of the stream. At 1.9 miles, you encounter a junction with a road to your left that descends to Virginia Creek and then follows the stream. If you tire of the walk up the main road, as an option you could follow this road next to the creek for 2 ½ miles to its end and then head cross country for the remaining 1 ¼ miles to Virginia Lakes.

Remaining on the main road, you cross into Forest Service land and soon after the amount of pine and aspen increases. As you continue the steady ascent, Dunderberg Peak seems to loom larger with each step. At 4.0 miles you reach a junction with Dunderberg Meadow Road heading north to connections with the Green Creek Road and, ultimately, US 395.

Beyond the junction, your rate of ascent eases. As you near a large hump of rock on the left, you begin to see cabins through the trees to your right, a clear indication that the lakes are not too much farther. Continue along the main road past the cabins and a road to Trumbull Lake, reaching the largest of the Virginia Lakes at 5 ¾ miles.

Summer Trailhead sign

The lake enjoys a very pretty setting, nestled beneath the open rugged slopes that rise up to 11,797-foot. Black Mountain. A block restroom building is near the lakeshore, but may be locked during winter. For additional picturesque views, Red Lake is just ¼ mile directly south and Blue Lake is a similar distance northwest. For more options see FYI below.

FYI: Most parties are content with the 5 ¾ mile journey to Virginia Lake, but for those with more ambitious desires, there are a number of additional lakes situated around the basin and farther up the Virginia Creek drainage. A 1 ½-mile trip extension up the route of the hikers' trail will take visitors to Blue, Cooney and Frog lakes. Another 3 ¼ miles of steep climbing over rugged terrain lead to Summit Lake, perched at the very crest of the Sierra on the northeastern boundary of Yosemite National Park. A journey to Summit Lake is for experienced parties in excellent condition only, but the lake provides an excellent base camp for a multi-day winter trip into this seldom-visited area.

Warm-ups: See Trip 30.

Trip 33

DUNDERBERG PEAK

Duration: Full day
Distance: 14 miles round trip
Difficulty: Extreme
Elevation: 8260/12374
Maps: 22; *Lundy & Dunderberg Peak* 7.5' quadrangles, (provisional),
1994
Hoover Wilderness, Toiyabe & Inyo National Forests, 1987

Introduction: The complete journey to the 12,374-foot summit of Dunderberg Peak requires plenty of stamina and a good dose of skill as well. Just reaching the base of the 2625-foot climb requires a 5 ½-mile snowshoe along the Virginia Lakes Road. Once the real climb begins, all that elevation must be overcome in a mere 1 ½ miles. This is definitely a trip reserved for snowshoers who are in excellent condition and possess mountaineering abilities. They must be prepared for an assortment of conditions on the south-facing slopes of the peak as well (see FYI). For those who meet these qualifications, the view from the summit is well worth all the effort. The unobstructed view takes in a vast section of the Sierra, as well as the unique setting of Mono Lake directly below to the east.

Trailhead: Follow directions in Trip 32 to the plowed parking area on Virginia Lakes Road.

Description: Follow directions in Trip 32 to near the 5 ½-mile mark on the Virginia Lakes trip description, near the turnoff to Trumbull Lake.

174

Leave the gentle grade of the road and head northwest to the prominent south ridge arcing down from Dunderberg Peak. Follow the ridge up the steep slopes on a continuous climb to the 12,115-foot saddle just east of the summit. Turn west and then northeast up the final slope to the top. A 360° panorama awaits.

FYI: Due to the south-facing exposure and a location along the eastern fringe of the Sierra, Dunderberg Peak maintains good snow conditions for only short periods of the winter. When you must make the full 5 ½-mile approach to the base of the peak, late winter and early spring offer extended hours of daylight, but the quality of the snow is apt to be marginal. Be prepared to face irregular snow conditions and bare patches en route to the summit.

Warm-ups: See Trip 30.

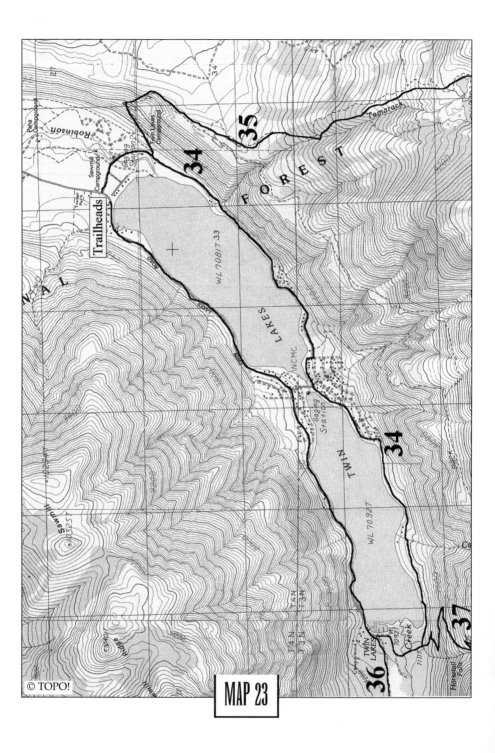

MAP 23

Trip 34

TWIN LAKES

Duration: ½ day to ¾ day
Distance: Varies—up to 9 ½ miles round trip
Difficulty: Easy
Elevation: 7085/7200
Maps: 23; *Twin Lakes* 7.5' quadrangle (provisional), 1990
   Hoover Wilderness, Toiyabe and Inyo National Forests, 1987

Introduction: An easy trip around the shore of a matching pair of beautiful lakes makes your journey around Twin Lakes a wonderful adventure. Most of the route follows the gentle grade of a snow-covered road, creating an ideal situation for beginning snowshoers. The scenery is quite attractive all the way around the lightly forested shoreline. The rugged mountains and the peaks 5000 vertical feet above lake create an alpine scene as dramatic as any in the Sierra.

A number of options are available for snowshoers to vary the length of their journey. From any point along the way, you can retrace your steps back to the car, satisfied with the delightful scenery en route. An isthmus between Twin Lakes allows the possibility of a shuttle trip of just over 2 ½ miles, while a pick-up at the north side of the upper lake at the end of Twin Lakes Road requires a 4 ¾-mile shuttle journey. For those without the benefit of a car shuttle, the full round trip necessitates a return of 3 ½ miles via the plowed Twin Lakes Road, or of 4 ¾ miles by following your tracks back to the car.

Whichever alternative you opt for, beneath the steep slopes above the lakes is no place to be when unstable snow conditions prevail. Such situations are not routine for areas in the eastern rain-shad-

Twin Lakes from trail

ow of the Sierra, but are not uncommon either, being most prevalent during and immediately after particularly heavy snowfalls.

How to get there: At the west end of the town of Bridgeport, following signs for Twin Lakes, turn south from US 395 onto Twin Lakes Road. Proceed westbound on two-lane asphalt for 9.5 miles to the left-hand turn onto South Twin Road. Mono County usually plows this road for a short distance, so park at the end of the plowed section of road as conditions allow.

Description: From your car, snowshoe along the extension of the roadway across the bridge over Robinson Creek and through Twin Lakes Campground. As you follow the road around the east end of the lake you have fine views south toward the serrated peaks forming Sawtooth Ridge.

Continue along the easy path of the roadway along the southeast shore of the first lake. Nearing the end of this lake, follow the road closest to the shoreline through a small subdivision of summer homes. At 2 ½ miles from Twin Lakes Road, you reach the narrow isthmus separating the two lakes. If you have arranged a car shuttle, you can end your trip by going across the isthmus another 500 feet to the north-shore road.

To extend your journey, remain on the snow-covered road and proceed along the southeast shore of the upper lake. Just beyond the 3-mile mark, the road ends and you must follow the shoreline without aid of a graded route. At the far end of the lake, turn north and snowshoe through Mono Village to the end of Twin Lakes Road, 4 ¾ miles from your starting point. Planning a pick-up at the road end will either save you from retracing your steps or save a 3 ½-mile walk along this road back to your car.

FYI: As you pass the cabins along the lake and through the Mono Village campground, please respect the rights of property owners.

Warm-ups: For breakfast and lunch, you can't go wrong with Hays Street Cafe, at the corner of US 395 and Hays Street in Bridgeport. Meals are medium-priced and are made from fresh ingredients. Open every day but Monday during winter, the restaurant hours are 7 A.M. to 1 P.M. Call (760) 932-7141 for more information. Like other cafes along this stretch of 395, the Hays Street Cafe is subject to periodic closures in winter.

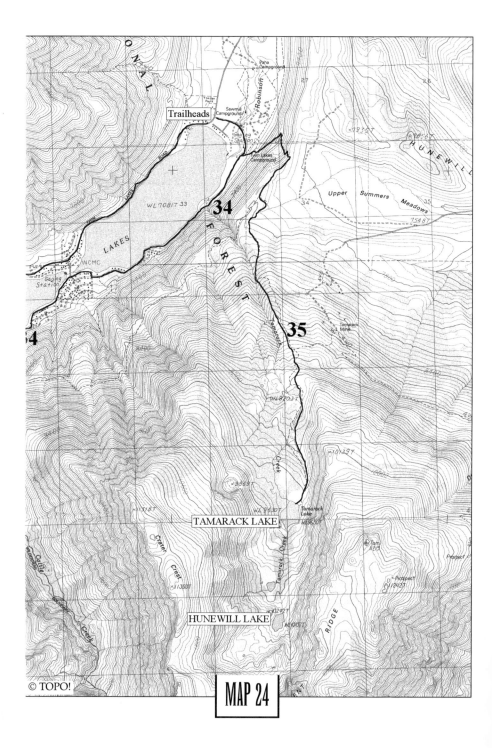

Trailheads

34

35

LAKES

FOREST

Upper Summers Meadows

TAMARACK LAKE

HUNEWILL LAKE

© TOPO!

MAP 24

TWIN LAKES TO TAMARACK LAKE

Duration: Full day
Distance: 9 miles round trip
Difficulty: Moderate
Elevation: 7100/9650
Maps: 24; *Twin Lakes & Dunderberg Peak* 7.5' quadrangles (provisional), 1990, 1994
Hoover Wilderness, Toiyabe and Inyo National Forests, 1987

Introduction: While relative solitude is nearly a foregone conclusion for trips around the Twin Lakes region, this trip to Tamarack Lake should provide a nearly ironclad guarantee of having the area all to yourself. The appearance of the initial climb across the steep wall of the canyon might deter the few winter recreationists who are up to the challenge. However, don't let looks fool you, since the climb across the steep wall of the canyon follows the moderate path of the summer trail, and the steepest part of the climb lasts only 1 ¼ miles.

Once you reach Tamarack Lake, you will be glad you endured the climb, as the picturesque lake is set in a lovely basin below the rocky cliffs of Monument Ridge.

How to get there: Follow directions in Trip 34.

Description: From your parking spot, follow the snow-covered road across the bridge over Robinson Creek and into the campground. About 50 feet before the second brick restroom in Twin Lakes

181

Campground, approximately ½ mile from Twin Lakes Road, is a sign on your left marking the Tamarack Lake trailhead.

At the sign, leave the road and follow the alignment of the trail as it makes a moderate climb angling northeast across the hillside. Unless the snowpack is abundant, the best route is to try to follow the trail, as the hillside is covered with sagebrush and other tall shrubs typical of the eastern Sierra. After a protracted climb, the trail does make a few switchbacks en route to the lip of Robinson Creek canyon. If following the path of the trail becomes difficult, select a route that heads toward the top of the hillside that avoids the worst of the brush.

Once you reach the crest, 1 ¼ miles from Twin Lakes Road, the grade of ascent abates. From this spot you also have a fine view of expansive Upper Summers Meadows, which would appear to be a fine location for skiers and snowshoers to practice their technique, if not for the fact that it is private land. From the ridge you also have fine views of Twin Lakes, Sawtooth Ridge and the surrounding peaks.

Turn southwest and follow the lip of the canyon around the meadows. After ½ mile of relatively gentle snowshoeing, turn south and head up the open slope towards the Tamarack Creek drainage. As you draw near the creek, avoid dropping into the canyon, as the drainage is steep and choked with trees and other vegetation. With the added elevation come fine views behind you of Bridgeport Valley, Bridgeport Lake and the Sweetwater Mountains.

Paralleling the creek, climb moderately above the lip of the canyon through a light forest of mountain mahogany. Continue to climb, now moderately steeply, along the east side of the drainage until you enter the middle section of the canyon, where the ascent eases, 3 ¼ miles from the car. Here you will find the open meadow containing the frozen pond shown on the *Twin Lakes* topo map.

Now you can follow the creek bed as it climbs more gently toward Tamarack Lake. After another 1 ¼ miles and 400 feet of elevation, you reach the north shore of lovely Tamarack Lake.

FYI: For a slightly more strenuous challenge, continuing another ½ mile beyond Tamarack Lake will take you to scenic Hunewill Lake,

Snowshoer in Upper Summer Meadow

nestled directly below Monument Ridge. The *Dunderberg Peak* topo map is necessary only for the extension to Hunewill Lake.

Warm-ups: The historic Bridgeport Inn, built as the Leavitt House in 1877, offers travelers passing through Bridgeport the opportunity for fine meals in the quaint dining room—breakfast, lunch, and dinner. O'Nolans Pub, across the entry hall from the dining room, has an excellent selection of libations to please the most sophisticated palate. Unfortunately, like many of the restaurants along this stretch of US 395, the Bridgeport Inn closes for part of the winter. Call (760) 932-7380 for more information.

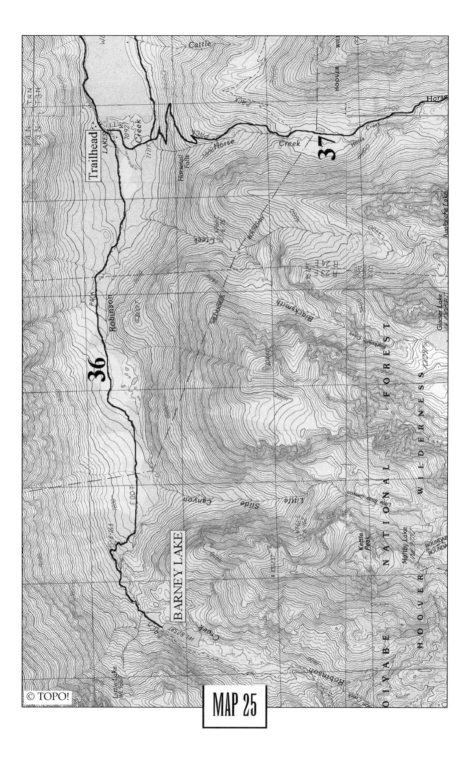

MAP 25

Trip 36

TWIN LAKES TO BARNEY LAKE

Duration: ¾ day
Distance: 8 miles round trip
Difficulty: Moderate
Elevation: 7120/8260
Maps: 25; *Buckeye Ridge* 7.5' quadrangle, 1990 (provisional)
      Hoover Wilderness, Toiyabe & Inyo National Forests, 1987

Introduction: The trip up Robinson Creek is a mellow stroll through light forest and open meadows. Only the last ¾ mile up to Barney Lake gains any significant elevation. The setting of the canyon is quite attractive, the tall ridges culminating in higher mountains like Robinson, Victoria, Hunewill and Kettle peaks. The beautiful scenery of the canyon is exceeded only by the lake itself, perched in a rocky bowl and surrounded by snowy ridges.

Although the terrain is easy for the most part, the area is no place to be when avalanche conditions are severe. Even your car is not safe under these circumstances if you park below the steep hillsides flanking Twin Lakes. If road conditions prevent you from driving all the way to Mono Village at the west end of the second lake, choose your location well to avoid potential slides. Proceed up the canyon away from the lakes only when the snow is stable.

One can savor the spectacular scenery on the drive into Twin Lakes, with the Sawtooth Ridge rising ruggedly over the expansive ranches of Bridgeport Valley. Unfortunately, you won't be able to see much of Sawtooth Ridge on the trip to Barney Lake, as the steep canyon walls block the views.

185

Barney Lake

Trailhead: At the west end of the town of Bridgeport, following signs for Twin Lakes, turn south from US 395 onto Twin Lakes Road. Proceed westbound on two-lane asphalt for 12.7 miles, past both Twin Lakes, to the end of the road at the entrance to Mono Village (Twin Lakes Resort). Park along the side of the road as conditions allow.

     If snow prevents you from reaching the resort entrance by car, you must park back down the road and hike to the road end. In this case, make sure you park in an area that is not prone to snowslides or avalanches.

Description: You begin your excursion by passing through Mono Village, following a route from the entrance station marked by red metal rectangles attached to trees. Continuing through the campground, you proceed through light pine forest along the right-hand (north) edge of a meadow. Just before the road meets Robinson Creek, your route bears right to follow above the creek on a moderate climb through mixed forest. The grade of ascent quickly becomes mild as you head up the canyon.

Eventually, you break out of the trees to a fine view up the canyon and continue a mild ascent through typical eastern Sierra vegetation, with sagebrush the dominant shrub. Farther along, you pass through scattered forest again, emerging to an excellent view of Little Slide Canyon and Kettle Peak to the south. The terrain remains relatively mild until you reach steeper slopes near the head of the canyon.

Where the terrain becomes steeper, you must work your way up the slope near the creek. During periods of adequate snowcover, you can hike directly up the hillside, but in times of less snow the route of the trail may provide easier passage through the thick brush. After approximately ¾ mile of moderate climbing, the terrain levels off just before Barney Lake. Make the short, easy stroll through pine forest over to the north shore of the lake.

Barney Lake is set in a deep-walled rock basin, overshadowed by the mass of Crown Point farther up the canyon. Scattered trees and steep, snow-covered granite slopes create a very picturesque setting, well-suited for a leisurely break or a lunch stop. Unless the lure of adventures farther up the canyon entices you to extend your journey, retrace your steps back to Twin Lakes.

FYI: While extending your trip farther up the canyon to either Robinson or Peeler lake is possible, the terrain is much steeper, requiring a lot more time and effort than the trip to Barney Lake.

Warm-ups: See Trips 34 and 35.

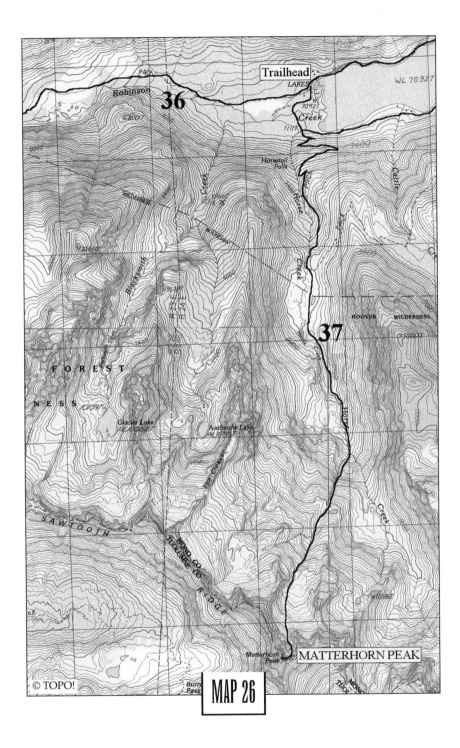

MAP 26

MATTERHORN PEAK

Duration: Full day or overnight
Distance: 10 miles round trip
Difficulty: Extreme
Elevation: 7095/12279
Maps: 26; *Buckeye Ridge, Twin Lakes & Matterhorn Peak* 7.5' quadrangles (provisional), 1990
   Hoover Wilderness, Toiyabe & Inyo National Forests, 1987

Introduction: Although it hardly resembles its Swiss counterpart, Matterhorn Peak presents a dramatic profile in the eastern Sierra sky. Anchoring the southeast end of rugged Sawtooth Ridge, Matterhorn rises over 5000 feet above Twin Lakes in less than 3 ½ airline miles, its lofty summit pyramid towering over the landscape of northeast Yosemite. A coveted ascent in summer, Matterhorn presents winter and spring climbers with the temptations of a demanding challenge and a superb view. Accomplished skiers are drawn to perhaps the best ski descent in the entire Sierra.

   Any attempt on this peak demands stamina, technical skill, and backcountry savvy. In actuality, the ascent is more of a mountain climb than a purely snowshoe adventure, requiring that you be skilled in the arts of using an ice axe and handling Class 3 climbing. A winter or early spring ascent during a year of average snowfall will necessitate the use of snowshoes (or skis) for the approach and the most of the ascent. Once at the base of the east couloir, the real climbing occurs over the next 800 vertical feet as you must climb a steep, snow-filled gully to the east ridge and then scramble over rocks on the southeast face to the top.

Two other factors that must be considered when contemplating a climb of Matterhorn Peak are the current avalanche conditions and the amount of daylight. Much of the route passes through steep terrain, which is no place to be when the avalanche danger is high. Most parties plan their attempts for early spring, when the snow is usually more consolidated. Springtime also sees longer days, and even the strongest party will need a full day to complete the climb and return to the starting point before dark. Don't forget to pack your headlamp or flashlight just in case the sun sets before you finish the trip. If you want to spread the ascent over two days, camping along Horse Creek or above is possible at a variety of locations.

If you are fortunate enough to attempt the trip on a clear day, the scenery is dramatic and the view from the summit is incredible. If you have room in your pack, take along a small-scale map of Yosemite and the surrounding peaks so you can identify the myriad summits stretching out to the north and south.

Trailhead: Follow directions in Trip 35. If your trip will be occurring

Rest stop below summit, Matterhorn Peak

after opening day of fishing season, you can park for free in the day-use parking area at Mono Village.

Description: Follow the blue rectangular markers through the campground at Mono Village to the bridge across Robinson Creek. You then follow a wide path on a short climb through more campsites to a footbridge across Horse Creek. From the crossing, wind along the creek momentarily before you turn south and climb up the hillside, quickly passing the wilderness trailhead sign.

From the sign, your moderate climb begins in earnest as you follow the Horse Creek Trail on a series of long switchbacks across the steep southern wall of the canyon east of the creek. At the second switchback, near the ½-mile mark, you encounter Horse Creek again, where you have a fine view of the tumbling cascade. Eventually, the trail curves into the Horse Creek drainage and follows above the creek on a southerly course. Farther up the drainage you come to an extraordinary view of Horsetail Falls spilling over the rock face of the lower canyon, with the high peaks of Sawtooth Ridge piercing the skies far above.

You continue along the trail as it makes an ascending traverse up the east side of the canyon and then comes alongside the creek above the falls. After the trail makes a sharp dogleg ascent, 2 miles from the parking area, you encounter a junction with a trail heading east toward Cattle Canyon. Above the junction, you follow the path across the nearly level floor of a ½-mile-long basin dotted with lodgepole pines. Next to the meandering creek, you will find a number of pleasant campsites nestled beneath the pines.

Beyond the nearly flat basin, your route resumes the climb up the drainage. The official course of the trail follows a continuously ascending path cut into the east side of the rocky slope above the creek. However, if this trail is snow-covered, you will find easier travel near the bottom of the canyon just east of the creek. Continue up the canyon, heading toward the saddle directly ahead.

The standard route of ascent for Matterhorn Peak follows a course to the top of the saddle. From there, turn southwest below a steep ridge to your right. Climb alongside the base of this ridge until you find a convenient point from which to make an ascent up to its crest. Once

Matterhorn Peak from trail

at the top, you can follow the apex of the ridge toward the bowl below the face of Matterhorn Peak.

A more direct, although slightly steeper, line of ascent avoids the longer climb to the saddle by climbing one of the gullies just past the pronounced rock outcropping near the 3 ¼-mile point. Finding your way across Horse Creek may present the greatest challenge if your visit coincides with the spring runoff. Once across the main branch of Horse Creek, make the steep climb up the gully, which carries a tributary stream. Continue directly up the cleft, passing a frozen tarn at 10,500-foot (campsites here) to the bowl below the northeast face of Matterhorn Peak.

By either approach, you must drop into the bowl and then climb up the glacier (technically a permanent snowfield) to the base of the east couloir. Ascend the steep couloir to the crest of the east ridge and then scramble up the rocks of the southeast face to the summit. Excellent views await you!

FYI: Expert backcountry or randonnee skiers and snowboarders will want to pack along the appropriate equipment for their descent. Horse Creek canyon offers some of the best skiing in all of the Sierra, and good weather over springtime weekends usually sees a number of parties cavorting across the slopes.

Warm-ups: After opening day of fishing season, you can grab a burger or a brew in the cafe at Mono Village. Otherwise try one of the establishments in Bridgeport in Trips 34 and 35.

Climbers on Matterhorn Peak

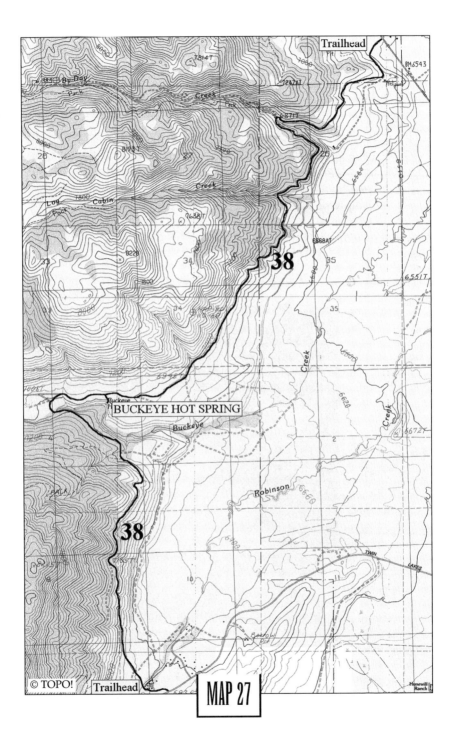

Trailhead

By Day
Park
Creek
Fork
8711T

26

38

6868AT

35

6551T

Creek

6620

Creek

BUCKEYE HOT SPRING

Buckeye

Buckeye

2

6672T

Robinson

38

TWIN
LAKES

© TOPO!

Trailhead

MAP 27

Trip 38

BUCKEYE HOT SPRINGS

Duration: ¾ day
Distance: 6 ¾ miles round trip from Twin Lakes Road
9 miles round trip from US 395
Difficulty: Easy to moderate
Elevation: 6845/7145/6930 from Twin Lakes Road
6565/7030/6930 from US 395
Maps: 27; *Twin Lakes & Mt. Jackson* 7.5' quadrangle (provisional), 1990
Hoover Wilderness, Toiyabe & Inyo National Forests, 1987

Introduction: For many, an ideal part of a successful snowshoe out-ing would be to bask in the mineral waters of a hot spring. On this journey, you can experience such a reward as a destination by travel-ing one of these routes to Buckeye Hot Springs, where two primitive pools offer snowshoers a brief respite from the frigid temperatures of winter. However, for this trip to be at its best, despite the relatively low elevation and a location well into the eastern rainshadow of the Sierra crest, excellent snow conditions are necessary.

As with many eastern Sierra trailheads, parking can be a prob-lem, particularly just after storms, although that's when the snow conditions are most likely to be the best for this particular trip. If you can't obtain a decent spot for your vehicle along the shoulder of Twin Lakes Road, you may have to chose the beginning point on US 395. Both routes are easy to follow as they utilize roads, and both are mildly graded as well. However, the trip from US 395, while provid-ing surer parking, is about a mile longer and has a greater chance of poor snow conditions at the start.

Whichever way you decide to go, don't forget a towel.

Trailhead: TWIN LAKES ROAD: At the west end of the town of Bridgeport, following signs for Twin Lakes, turn south from US 395 onto Twin Lakes Road. Proceed westbound on two-lane asphalt 7.6 miles to the junction with Buckeye Road, near a sign for DOC & AL'S RESORT. Park near the junction as conditions allow, making sure you do not park in the plowed section of Buckeye Road (you may be towed if you park there). If a suitable site can't be found, consider the longer option from US 395.

US 395: On US Highway 395, find the signed turnoff 3.8 miles northwest of the town of Bridgeport, marked: BUCKEYE CG 6, TWIN LAKES ROAD 8. Park as snow allows, either up the road or alongside the highway shoulder.

Description: TWIN LAKES ROAD: Head down Buckeye Road and immediately encounter a **Y**-junction. Take the left-hand branch, as the right-hand road leads into Doc & Al's Resort. You proceed along the road through widely scattered pines and sagebrush. As you work your way past the resort, the road curves and crosses Robinson Creek on an old wooden bridge. Past the bridge, you begin a steady climb across the hillside. Initially you have nice views of a part of Sawtooth Ridge and across Bridgeport Valley to the Sweetwater Mountains.

As you continue to climb steadily, you leave the views of Sawtooth Ridge behind, but the views across the valley continue to improve. At 1 ½ miles you begin a lengthy descent, eventually curving into the Buckeye Creek drainage. Cross Buckeye Creek on a wooden bridge at 2 ½ miles, and make a short climb up to a **Y**-junction.

At the **Y**, bear to the right, following directions on a sign marked 395. You proceed along this road for ½ mile to a large, sloping clearing. Just below this clearing is Buckeye Hot Springs, right above Buckeye Creek.

The hardest part of your journey will be descending the steep hillside to the two pools next to the creek. Be alert as you cross the slippery slope down to the level of the creek. Now you can enjoy the hot spring-fed water of the two shallow pools. The water from the hot springs runs down the hillside and drips over the rock above into these pools, creating a water temperature well-suited to taking the chill out of a normal winter's day.

US 395: From the highway, follow Forest Service Road 017 as it heads southwest before it bends sharply southeast. The grade increases as you follow the road around a hill on a moderate climb through classic eastern Sierra sagebrush. The ascent eases as you bend west into the drainage of By-Day Creek. In scattered pines, you cross the creek just past the 1 ¼-mile mark and head out of the drainage and around the hillside to the next stream, Cabin Creek. You follow the nearly level road across the creek at 2 ¼ miles and then on a mild traverse across the hillside.

The second half of your journey takes you on a mild, uneventful climb across the hillside and into the Buckeye Creek drainage. Away from the two previous creeks, you find yourself once again in mostly sagebrush terrain. The only trees that break up the slope are widely scattered pinyon pines. Eventually, you reach the open slope above the hot springs and descend carefully down the steep slopes to the creek.

FYI: If you find the pools are too hot for your preference, you can regulate the temperature somewhat by unplugging the upstream pipe which allows cold water from Buckeye Creek to mix with the water in the pools. Be extremely careful not to pollute the springs, pools or creek, leaving a pleasant environment for those who come after you.

If you wish to extend your journey, continuing west up Buckeye Canyon provides opportunities for snowshoeing the gentle terrain along Buckeye Creek through extensive stands of aspen.

The *Mt. Jackson* map is necessary only for the beginning part of the trip starting at US 395.

Warm-ups: See trips 34-35.

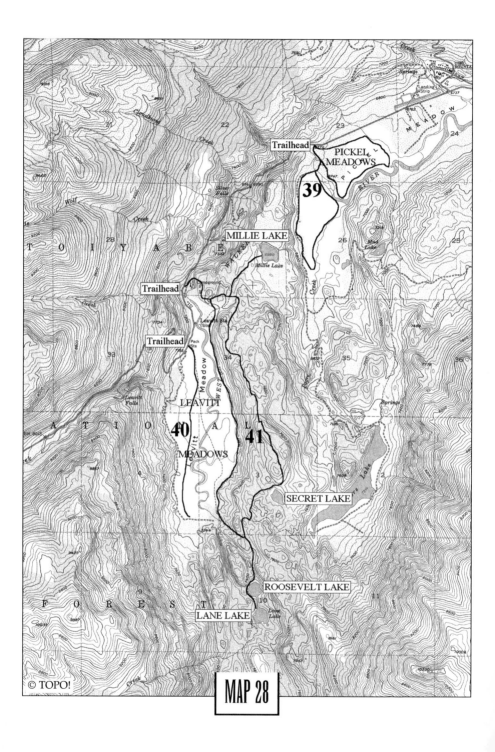

MAP 28

Trip 39

PICKEL MEADOWS

Duration: ½ day
Distance: Varies
Difficulty: Easy
Elevation: 6740/6760
Maps: 28; *Pickel Meadow* 7.5' quadrangle, 1954 (photo revised 1978)
    Hoover Wilderness, Toiyabe & Inyo National Forests, 1987

Introduction: The flat expanse of Pickel Meadows provides beginners with an ideal setting for getting used to a new activity. Tailoring wanderings to suit your desires is quite easy. Reaching the West Walker River requires only a ¼ mile of travel, while circling the meadows could result in a 4 ½-mile loop.

Rimmed by snow-clad ridges, the meadows are quite picturesque when blanketed with a fresh layer of powder. Located in the rainshadow of the eastern fringe of the Sierra, Pickel Meadows is best visited in years of heavy snowpack

Aside from seeing soldiers from the Mountain Warfare Training Center across the highway, you should have the area pretty much to yourself, as the Sonora Pass Road is closed in the winter, preventing easy access from the valleys of California.

How to get there: Follow US 395 to the junction with Highway 108 and proceed west on Sonora Pass Highway 108. At 3.6 miles, you will reach the east edge of the Mountain Warfare Training Center across from Pickel Meadows. Technically, this is as far as Cal Trans plows the highway in heavy snow years. However, during most years, continuing another 1.3 miles to the locked gate should not be a problem. This gate officially closes the road in winter. Park alongside the road wherever conditions allow.

Description: From your parking spot, proceed onto the meadows and snowshoe wherever you desire. Pickel Meadows is a large open plain providing easy snowshoeing alongside the West Walker River. If you can find a way across the river at the west end of the meadows, extending your wanderings a mile or so up Poore Creek is possible before the terrain becomes steeper.

FYI: Continuous activities occur in and around the MWTC—don't be alarmed by their maneuvers.

Warm-ups: Good luck! Unless you stored a thermos of hot coffee or soup in your car, the closest place to acquire hot food or drink is many miles away. Heading south on 395, your nearest watering holes are in Bridgeport (see Trips 34 & 35). Traveling north, you have to journey to Coleville or Walker, where just about everything closes down in the winter, or all the way to Topaz Lake or Gardnerville, Nevada.

Trip 40

LEAVITT MEADOWS

Duration: ½ - ¾ day
Distance: Varies
Difficulty: Easy
Elevation: 7150/7175
Maps: 28; *Pickel Meadow* 7.5 minute quadrangle, 1954 (photo revised 1978)
   Hoover Wilderness, Toiyabe & Inyo National Forest, 1987

Introduction: Leavitt Meadows is 400 feet higher and 2 miles west of Pickel Meadows, which is enough of a change to produce better snow conditions. However, you have to walk an extra 2 ¼ miles to get there if the road is not passable. Once at the meadows, you can follow the course of the West Walker River flowing over a level plain surrounded by snowy ridges. Views of higher peaks up the canyon beckon travelers to extend their wanderings.

   Leavitt Meadows is 2 miles long and ½ mile wide, allowing you to vary the length of your trip as you wish. As at Pickel Meadows, the flat terrain is well-suited for beginners and for more experienced snowshoers looking for an easy trip.

How to get there: Follow directions in Trip 39 to the east edge of the Mountain Warfare Training Center across from Pickel Meadows. Technically, this is as far as Cal Trans plows the highway in heavy snow years. However, continuing another 1.3 miles and parking near the locked gate across the highway should not be a problem. Although this gate officially closes the road in winter, in drier years driving around the gate and continuing to the pack station at Leavitt Meadows, 7.2 miles from US 395, may be possible.

Description: If you have to park at the gate, snowshoeing the road for 2 ¼ miles to the Leavitt Meadows Pack Station will be necessary. Follow the highway on a winding climb, quickly crossing Wolf Creek 0.3 mile from the gate. As you ascend there are nice views across the canyon to the snow-covered slope above the West Walker River. Approximately 1 ½ miles from the gate, you begin a mild descent through a light forest of pine down to Leavitt Meadows. Continue along the road past a campground and the backpacker trailhead to easy access to the meadows near the pack station.

In Leavitt Meadows you head south along the West Walker River as it winds sinuously through the 2-mile long plain. Since there is no easy way across the river, your wanderings will be confined to the west side of the basin. The scenery is very pleasant and the level terrain is certainly not taxing.

FYI: Finding reliable information on the condition of the road past the MWTC is difficult. Technically, the road is closed once Cal Trans locks the gate, although you may still be able to safely drive the road during light snow years. Unfortunately, you most likely will have to drive to the gate and see for yourself whether further progress is possible, rather than obtaining the information ahead of time.

Warm-ups: See Trip 39.

LEAVITT MEADOWS TO MILLIE, SECRET, ROOSEVELT & LANE LAKES

Duration: ¾ day
Distance: 6 ¼ miles loop trip
      1 mile round trip extension to Millie Lake
      1 ¼ miles round trip extension to Roosevelt & Lane Lakes
Difficulty: Moderate
Elevation: 7120/7450
Maps: 28; *Pickel Meadow* 7.5' quadrangle, 1954 (photo revised 1978)
      Hoover Wilderness, Toiyabe & Inyo National Forests, 1987

Introduction: This trip from Leavitt Meadows allows snowshoers to sample up to four secluded lakes on a 6 ¼-to-8 ½-mile loop trip, provided you can drive all the way to Leavitt Meadows Campground. If the highway from Pickel Meadows is impassable due to too much snow, you will have to add another 2 ¼ miles to your journey.

    The terrain along the route is relatively gentle, requiring only short sections of moderate climbing. Routefinding is relatively simple to Millie and Secret lakes through the dry, open vegetation typical of the eastern Sierra. The route to Roosevelt and Lane lakes requires a bit more skill due to increased forest cover and more involved terrain. In addition to the lakes, you have the opportunity to snowshoe the length of scenic Leavitt Meadows near the end of the loop. The open terrain along the top of the ridge above the meadows provide excellent views of the eastern Sonora Pass region, including glimpses of Tower and Forsyth peaks.

How to get there: Follow directions in Trip 40 as far as the Leavitt Meadows Campground and park on the side of the road.

Description: Follow the access road through the campground to the bridge across the West Walker River. Once across the bridge you make a short climb and wrap around some low hills on a moderate ascent. Passing through a light covering of pine, juniper and mountain mahogany you come to a signed trail junction with the West Walker River Trail, 0.4 mile from the road. Bear left at the junction and continue to climb up to a small meadow, approximately ½ mile from the highway. To visit Millie Lake, head northeast from this meadow on a short ascent and then drop down moderately, reaching the shoreline in ½ mile. Irregularly shaped Millie Lake sits in a shallow, sagebrush-lined bowl which grants a nice view of Pickel Meadows 250 feet below.

Continuing along the route of the Leavitt Meadow High Trail, you make a moderate ascent toward the crest of the ridge. You can either snowshoe directly along the crest or follow the less undulating route of the trail along the west side of the ridge. Proceeding through widely scattered forest along the top of the ridge, you have nice views of Pickel Meadows and the Sweetwater Mountains to the northeast, Leavitt Meadows surrounded by snow-capped ridges directly below, and Tower and Forsyth peaks to the south. Just before the terrain drops sharply to Secret Lake, 2 ¼ miles from the road, you have a glimpse of lengthy Poore Lake to the east.

You drop down through light forest to the northeast shore of Secret Lake, 2 ½ miles from the campground. The small lake is surrounded by a rocky shoreline, with steep cliffs on the opposite side forming a scenic backdrop.

Your route climbs away from Secret Lake over a shoulder and then begins a mild descent. You reach a junction ¾ mile from the lake, where you have a choice between a round-trip journey to Roosevelt and Lane lakes, and a direct route to Leavitt Meadows. The jaunt to the lakes will add 1 ¼ miles to your trip.

To get to Roosevelt Lake, descend mildly south, eventually passing through a gulch between cliffs to reach the north shore. A small isthmus separates Roosevelt Lake from its southern twin, Lane Lake. In the summer these two shallow lakes are heavily visited, but in winter you are likely to be completely alone. Now retrace your steps back to the last junction.

From the junction, you can simply retrace your steps back to the road or bear northwest and follow the route of the loop trip toward Leavitt Meadows. Once at the meadows, head along the east edge for 1 ¾ miles, with the meandering West Walker River to your left. At the north end of the meadows, curve around toward the signed trail junction, 0.4 mile from the highway. From the junction, reverse your steps back to the car.

FYI: The West Walker River provides plenty of opportunities for longer trips. However, make sure you know the weather forecast before venturing into the backcountry. Your vehicle could easily become irretrievable until spring if buried by a sudden snowstorm, necessitating a long walk home.

Warm-ups: See Trip 39.

IMPORTANT PHONE NUMBERS

Avalanche Conditions	(530) 587-2158
Emergency	911
Friends of Yosemite	(415) 434-1782
Highway Patrol (Bishop)	(760) 873-3531
Road Conditions	(800) 427-7623

Sheriff

Mono County	(760) 932-7549
Yosemite Association	(209) 379-2646
Yosemite Institute	(209) 379-9511

Yosemite NP—Campground Reservations	(800) 436-7275
Yosemite NP—Cross Country Ski Center	(209) 372-8444
Yosemite NP—Curry Village Ice Skating Rink	(209) 372-8341
Yosemite NP—General Information—recorded	(209) 372-0200
Yosemite NP—General Information—live operator .	(900) 454-YOSE
Yosemite NP—Lodging Reservations	(559) 252-4848
Yosemite NP—Road Conditions (24 hour)	(209) 372-0200
Yosemite NP—Ski Conditions (Badger Pass)	(209) 372-1000
Yosemite NP—Snow Conditions (24 hour)	(209) 372-1000
Yosemite NP—Wilderness Permit Reservations	(209) 372-0740

IMPORTANT WEB SITES

Ansel Adams Gallery	.anseladams.com
Fresno Yosemite International Airport . . .	.fresno.com/fly fresno
National Park Service—Yosemite	.nps.gov/yose/
United States Geological Survey	.usgs.gov/
Weather Channel	.weather.com
Wilderness Press	.wildernesspress.com
Wildflower Productions (TOPO)	.topo.com
YNP Reservations	.reservations.nps.gov

Yosemite Area Traveler Information . . . . .yosemite.com
Yosemite Association . . . . .yosemite.org
Yosemite Concession Services . . . . .yosemitepark.com
Yosemite Fund . . . . .yosemitefund.org
Yosemite-Sierra Visitors Bureau . . . . .yosemite-sierra.org
Yosemite West . . . . .yosemitelodging.com

FOREST SERVICE LISTINGS

Stanislaus National Forest

Forest Supervisor's Office
19777 Greenley Road
Sonora, CA 95370
(209) 532-3671

Calaveras Ranger District
Highway 4/PO Box 500
Hathaway Pines, CA 95321
(209) 795-1381

Groveland Ranger District
24525 Old Highway 120
Groveland, CA 95321
(209) 962-7825

Mi-Wok Ranger District
Highway 108/PO Box 100
Mi-Wuk Village, CA 95346
(209) 586-3234

Summit Ranger District
Highway 108
#1 Pinecrest Lake Road
Pinecrest, CA 95364
(209) 965-3434

Sierra National Forest

Supervisor's Office
1600 Tollhouse Road
Clovis, CA 93612
(209) 297-0706

Mariposa Ranger District
41969 Highway 41
Oakhurst, CA 93644
(209) 683-4665

Toiyabe National Forest

Supervisor's Office
1200 Franklin Way
Sparks, NV 89431
(775) 331-6444 or 355-5302

Bridgeport Ranger District
PO Box 595
Bridgeport, CA 93517
(619) 932-7070

Inyo National Forest

Forest Supervisor's Office
873 North Main
Bishop, CA 93514
(619) 873-2400

Mammoth Ranger District
PO Box 148
Mammoth Lakes, CA 93546
(619) 924-5500

Mono Lake Ranger District
PO Box 429
Lee Vining, CA 93541
(619) 647-3000

SNOWSHOE MANUFACTURERS

Atlas Snowshoe Co.
1830 Harrison Street
San Francisco, CA 94103
(800) 645-SHOE
fax: (415) 252-0354
atlasworld.com

C3
Carney Composites
6146 S. 350 West
Salt Lake City, UT 84107
(801) 281-1331
verts.com

K2
19215 Vashon Hwy SW
Vashon, Island, WA 98070
(800) 666-2579

Mountain Safety Research
PO Box 24547
Seattle, WA 98124
(800) 877-9677
(206) 624-7048
fax: (206) 224-6492
msrcorp.com

Northern Lites
1300 Cleveland Ave.
Wausau, WI 54401
(800) 360-LITE
fax: (715) 677-2776
northernlites.com

Redfeather
4955-D Peoria Street
Denver, CO 80239
(303) 375-0410
redfeather.com

Sherpa Snowshoes
444 S. Pine Street
Burlington, WI 53105
(800) 621-2277
fax: (414) 763-4506
email:
jeremy@sherpasnowshoes.com
sherpasnowshoes.com

TSL
PO Box 19754
Portland, OR 97280
(888) 782-2228

Tubbs Snowshoe Company
52 River Road
Stowe, VT 05672
(800) 882-2748
fax: (800) 253-9982
tubbssnowshoes.com

YubaShoes
161 Main Ave.
Sacramento, CA 95338
(800) 598-YUBA
(916) 920-5339
email: feedback@yubashoes.com
yubashoes.com

SUGGESTED READING

Browning, Peter. 1991. *Place Names of the Sierra Nevada*. Berkeley: Wilderness Press.

Browning, Peter. 1988. *Yosemite Place Names*. Lafayette, CA: Great West Books.

Bunnell, M.D., Lafayette Houghton. 1990. *Discovery of the Yosemite*. Yosemite National Park: Yosemite Association.

Darvill, M.D., Fred. 1998. *Mountaineering Medicine*. 14th Edition. Berkeley: Wilderness Press.

Farquhar, Francis. 1965. *History of the Sierra Nevada*. Berkeley: University of California Press.

Graydon, Don & Curt Hanson, editors. 1997. *Mountaineering: The Freedom of the Hills*. 6th Edition. Seattle: The Mountaineers.

LaChapelle, Ed. 1985. *ABC of Avalanche Safety*, 2nd Edition. Seattle: The Mountaineers.

Libkind, Marcus. 1985. *Ski Tours in the Sierra Nevada, Volume 2, Carson Pass, Bear Valley, Pinecrest*. Livermore, CA: Bittersweet Publishing Company.

Libkind, Marcus. 1985. *Ski Tours in the Sierra Nevada, Volume 3, Yosemite, Huntington & Shaver Lakes, Kings Canyon, Sequoia*. Livermore, CA: Bittersweet Publishing Company.

Morey, Kathy. 1996. *Hot Showers, Soft Beds, and Dayhikes in the Sierra. Walks and Strolls Near Lodgings*. Berkeley: Wilderness Press.

Muir, John. 1988. *The Yosemite*. San Francisco: Sierra Club.

O'Bannon, Allen & Mike Clelland. 1996. *Allen & Mike's Really Cool Backcountry Ski Book*. Evergreen, CO: Chockstone Press.

Prater, Gene. Edited by Dave Felkey. 1997. *Snowshoeing*. 4th Edition. Seattle: The Mountaineers.

Roper, Steve. 1976. *The Climber's Guide to the High Sierra*. San Francisco: Sierra Club.

Russell, Carl Parcher. 1992. *One Hundred Years in Yosemite. Omnibus Edition*. Yosemite National Park: Yosemite Association.

Sanborn, Margaret. 1989. *Yosemite. Its Discovery, Its Wonders and its People*. Yosemite National Park: Yosemite Association.

Schaffer, Jeffrey P. 1992. *Yosemite National Park*. 3rd Edition. Berkeley: Wilderness Press.

Schaffer, Jeffrey P. 1992. *Carson-Iceberg Wilderness*. 2nd Edition. Berkeley: Wilderness Press.

Schifrin, Ben. 1990. *Emigrant Wilderness and Northwestern Yosemite*. Berkeley: Wilderness Press.

Secor, R. J. 1992. *The High Sierra. Peaks, Passes, and Trails*. Seattle: The Mountaineers.

White, Michael C. 1997. *Nevada Wilderness Areas and Great Basin National Park*. Berkeley: Wilderness Press.

White, Michael C. 1998. *Snowshoe Trails of Tahoe*. Berkeley: Wilderness Press.

Wilkerson, M.D., James A. 1983. *Medicine for Mountaineering*. 2nd Edition. Seattle: The Mountaineers.

ACKNOWLEDGEMENTS

As with all of my writing projects, my first acknowledgement goes to my wife, Robin, who has believed in me since the very first time I made a feeble attempt to put my ideas on paper. Her continual support and encouragement have sustained me through yet another book. Not the least of her nearly endless contributions is the proofreading of my manuscript.

Thanks are also due to my publisher, Caroline Winnett, who had the original idea that spawned the *Snowshoe Trails* series and whose trust in me has been unwavering throughout our professional relationship, and to her father, Tom, for his typically excellent work on editing the manuscript. I would also like to thank all the folks at Wilderness Press who do such a fine job on my projects.

Winter is not the best time to be out in the backcountry alone and I have had the enormous privilege of quite a bit of company throughout the course of the field work for this book. First and foremost, I would like to thank my good friend Chris Taylor, who spent a quite a bit of time lifting my spirits amid the gray days of winter, not to mention saving me from the breaking of many miles of trail. Keith Catlin, my hiking and climbing partner of over 25 years, was a real joy to have along on a few trips, especially as we recalled the glory of our more youthful days in the Cascades. I was also fortunate to have the uplifting presence of another long-time friend, Dan Palmer, on some of the journeys to the eastern Sierra. After a number of cancellations due to poor weather, Mike Wilhelm finally did join me for an eastern Sierra trip late in the season. My niece, Carmel Snyder, was able to snowshoe one trip with me, as were Dave Miller, Dave Tompkins and Michelle Drake.

Many others provided technical support and answered a variety of questions. Thanks are extended to Mike Alger for once again digging up some weather data. A number of Forest Service and Park Service personnel were gracious enough to provide assistance from time to time, and even though I have forgotten most of their names, I appreciate greatly the help they extended to me.

Lastly, but most importantly, I would like to thank God for life itself, for creating such a magnificent area as Yosemite, and for allowing me the privilege to roam about in the midst of such beauty and then to write about what I found.

— Michael C. White

ABOUT THE MAPS IN THIS BOOK

The maps in this book were created using TOPO! Interactive Maps on CD-ROM from Wildflower Productions. Designed specifically for outdoor enthusiasts, TOPO! CD-ROMS are recognized as the best in digital navigation for backcountry snowshoeing, skiing, and snowboarding. TOPO! features detailed, accurate USGS maps enhanced with millions of digital elevation points. Powerful tools provide instant elevation profiles, real-time coordinates for GPS users, and extended capabilities for exploring, customizing, and printing seamless topographic maps.

This book was created using TOPO! *Yosemite, Mammoth, and Central Sierra Wilderness Areas*. In addition to the *Yosemite, Mammoth, and Central Sierra* area maps, Wildflower Productions offers interactive maps products for most recreational and metropolitan areas throughout the USA. To learn more about TOPO!, or to find a dealer near you, contact Wildflower Productions at (415) 558-8700. For product information, free upgrades and downloadable trail sets, visit www.topo.com.

For more information, contact:

Wildflower Productions
375 Alabama St., Suite 400
San Francisco, CA 94110
Phone: (415) 558-8700
Fax: (415) 558-9700
E-mail: *info@topo.com*
Web: http://www.topo.com

INDEX